PASSAGES OF THE SOUL

James Roose-Evans is one of Britain's most innovative theatre directors. His achievements as a director include his own adaptation of Helene Hanff's *84 Charing Cross Road*, which he directed on Broadway and in London's West End, winning awards on both sides of the Atlantic for Best Director and Best Play, as well as winning for its principal actors Best Actress and Best Actor awards. He directed the triumphant return to the West End of Sir John Gielgud in Hugh Whitemore's *The Best of Friends*, also starring Rosemary Harris and Ray McAnally. He directed Edwige Feuillère in the French production in Paris of the same play at the Comédie des Champs Elysées. He is the Founder of the Hampstead Theatre in London, and Founder and Director of The Bleddfa Trust – Centre for Caring and the Arts in the Welsh Marches.

He is the first British theatre director to be ordained a non-stipendiary priest, and has preached in Westminster Abbey. He is the author of many books including the classic *Experimental Theatre*, as well as other theatre books, and his own account of his spiritual journey, *Inner Journey, Outer Journey*. He wrote *Re:Joyce!*, an entertainment about Joyce Grenfell, especially for Maureen Lipman, which has had three sell-out seasons in the West End. He has also edited two best-selling books about Joyce Grenfell: *Darling Ma* and *The Time of My Life*.

He has been on the Faculty of the Julliard School of Music in New York and the Royal Academy of Dramatic Art in London; has been the Gian-Carlo Menotti Artist-in-Residence at Charleston, and Distinguished Visiting Fellow at Ohio State University. He has done a nationwide lecture tour of women's clubs in America, and led many workshops and summer schools there, as well as leading ritual workshops at the National Theatre Studio in London. He is a member of the Garrick Club and of the Dramatists' Club. He lives in Wales, Ireland and England, and continues to direct in the theatre.

By the same author

Directing a Play
Experimental Theatre
London Theatre
Inner Journey, Outer Journey
Darling Ma (ed.)
The Time of my Life (ed.)

CHILDREN'S BOOKS

The Adventures of Odd and Elsewhere
The Secret of the Seven Bright Shiners
Odd and the Great Bear
Elsewhere and the Gathering of the Clowns
The Return of the Great Bear
The Secret of Tippity Witchit
The Lost Treasure of Wales

PLAYS

84 Charing Cross Road
Cider with Rosie
Re: Joyce!
Augustus
A Pride of Players
The Little Clay Cart

CONTRIBUTIONS TO:

The Children's Book of Prayers
Prayers for the Day, BBC
England's Way
Actor Training 2

Passages of the Soul

Ritual Today

JAMES ROOSE-EVANS

ELEMENT
Shaftesbury, Dorset ● Rockport, Massachusetts
Brisbane, Queensland

Published in Great Britain in 1994 by
Element Books Limited
Longmead, Shaftesbury, Dorset

Published in the USA in 1994 by
Element, Inc.
42 Broadway, Rockport, MA 01966

Published in Australia in 1994 by
Element Books Limited for
Jacaranda Wiley Limited
33 Park Road, Milton, Brisbane, 4064

Cover design by Max Fairbrother
Design by Roger Lightfoot
Typeset by Footnote Graphics, Warminster, Wiltshire
Printed and bound in Great Britain by
Biddles Limited, Guildford & King's Lynn

British Library Cataloguing in Publication
data available

Library of Congress Cataloging in Publication
data available

ISBN 1–85230–474–X

Contents

The creative process, so far as we are able to follow it at all, consists in the unconscious activation of an archetypal image, and in elaborating and shaping this image into the finished work. . . By giving the image shape the artist translates it into the language of the present and so makes it possible for us to find our way back to the deepest springs of life. . .

Carl Jung

This book is dedicated
to the memory of
WENDY HALL
to whose generous friendship
and encouragement
I shall always be indebted.

Acknowledgements

Because this book is in many ways a summation of a major part of my life, I am indebted to so many who have both enriched and enabled me on my way, and to whom I shall always be grateful. They are: my first and main analyst, Dr Frans Elkisch, and Dr Masha Rollings who for a year in New York saw me weekly and never charged me; Martha Hill and Harold Gray of the Julliard School of Music, who first invited me to New York in 1955; Doris Humphrey, Alwin Nikolais, Murray Louis, John Martin, Craig Barton, Bruce Marks, Pearl Lang and Eileen Garrett, each of whom supported my work during that crucial year of exploration; and always Katherine and Henry Wells whose warmth of friendship sustained me then and now.

I would like also to thank Professor James Malcolm of the Theatre Department at Colorado College, Colorado Springs, for inviting me to teach a course on ritual; and Professor Reid Gilbert who secured me a Distinguished Visiting Fellowship in 1991 at Ohio State University so that I might do further research. My thanks to the Guild of Pastoral Psychology in London which invited me to give a paper on ritual; to Bani Shorter who invited me to give a paper on death and ritual for the Independent Group of Analytical Psychologists in London; Kathleen Raine for inviting me to write a paper on magic and enchantment for the Temenos Academy; Sue Higginson and Diane Borger of the National Theatre Studio in London for asking me to do a project on ritual; Anna Halprin of the Tamalpa Institute in California for flying me there to take part in the mountain ritual; Elin Dodson for allowing me to quote her *Simple Ritual for Coming Alive*; Jenny Pearson of *Sesame* who has encouraged me to lead a series of workshops for therapists; Judith Meikle for setting up the very first workshops I gave for therapists and psychotherapists; and, always, Dr Anthony Stevens for his constant encouragement and feedback.

The voices of many of those who have worked with me over the years are to be heard throughout this book, while several speak directly through the pages of their journals. These serve to highlight the importance of and the need for rituals in the lives of the young today, and I am indebted to them for allowing me to quote so freely. Somewhere Carl Jung wrote, 'No doubt we are right to open the ears and eyes of our young people to the wide world, but no one gives a thought to the necessity of adapting to the inner self, to the powers of the psyche, which are far mightier than the great powers of the earth.' My thanks therefore to: Anjali Biswas, Scott Phillips, Curt Alfrey, Roger Freeman, Kaizaad Kotwal, Lori, Monica, Paul, Sandra, Emily Stuart, Jennefer Hutzler, Carolyn Gracey and, above all, to Dickson Musslewhite whose journal is here included in its entirety.

I would like to thank Charlie and Sally Ware for allowing me to quote from their letters to me; Derek Shiel of the Men's Group in England who introduced me to the writings of Robert Bly; Jean Ridge who once spent three hours in Cork, photocopying the manuscript of this book – greater love hath no friend! and my editor, Ian Fenton, for his patience and percipience; Mary Fulton for her generous help. My thanks also to John Hencher for allowing me to describe his Easter ritual, as well as for his friendship and inspiration over the years; and lastly, Hywel Jones, my friend of thirty-five years, who has never ceased to challenge, stimulate, and support this creative work.

James Roose-Evans, 1993
Ballywilliam, County Cork

Introduction

It was in New York, in 1955–6, that I first began to explore theatre as ritual and ritual as theatre while I was teaching at the Julliard School of Music, working with a group of dancers, singers, musicians and one composer, to see how music, dance and drama might be integrated. For over forty years, alongside my other theatre work, I have continued to explore ritual and the need for ritual in society today, working in America, Britain, Finland and Greece. Many of those with whom I have worked have been professional actors, dancers and performers, whether at the Julliard in New York, the National Theatre Studio, the Actors' Centre or the Royal Academy of Dramatic Art in London. It was at the latter that I first taught Mike Leigh the hand ritual. In the past few years I have been asked to work with therapists and psychoanalysts. This I owe in part to Judith Meikle, to Jenny Pearson of *Sesame* and to Bani Shorter who has both challenged and encouraged me. Today, an average group at a workshop, is likely to contain a mix of professional performers, a travelling salesman and a computer specialist, as well as a growing number of therapists. What draws people from many backgrounds is the need, as one of them phrased it, 'to find meaningful and healing rituals'.

In 1981, while I was directing the world première of Helene Hanff's *84 Charing Cross Road*, which I had also adapted, I became the first British theatre director to be ordained a non-stipendiary priest of the Anglican Church, although my life remains in theatre, working as a director. In writing this book I have drawn occasionally upon certain experiences in my work as a priest, in the hope that this may stimulate others, of whatever religious affiliation, to be open to the creative exploration of ritual within their own tradition. But the main thrust of this book, and of the work, is towards those who do not belong to any specific religious tradition, who often have grave problems with existing structures and institutions, but who nonetheless have a surprising hunger for the things of the spirit, sensing that there is a spiritual dimension to life as well as a need to worship, and who struggle to find a way to express this. They are, to adapt a title of one of Carl Jung's best-known books, the modern men and women in search of a soul who, like Dickson Musslewhite at the close of this book, pledge themselves 'to search, to swim, to dive as deep as I can'.

The tragedy of so many people's lives is that suddenly, and often too late, they are aware of having wasted their lives, of never having fulfilled their potential. A woman once wrote to me, having heard me speak on television; she was sixty-two and referred to the fact that she had only six months left to live. 'I need spiritual and mental help,' she wrote. 'Till I heard you I was resigned to sitting it out to the end.' Her early letters were full of anger: towards God, the Church, the world. In the course of our correspondence she revealed that at the age of eighteen she had studied art but had then developed a mental block against it, being afraid to allow herself to be spontaneous because, as she expressed it, 'spontaneity is lovely but there is a risk'. And so, rather than take this risk, she repressed her rich creativity, denied her true self, and 'flung myself into secretarial work, changed jobs frequently and ended up with only a state pension. I am left with an ability to *feel* beauty in all its forms, but no ability now to pick up pencil or brush. Too diminished and mentally exhausted to *do*, I am left with a sense of having wasted my life.'

I wrote back asking her to do something: to go out and buy a child's box of paints and to sit down each day and paint, exactly like a child, whatever she was *feeling*, without any interference from her conscious critical self. About two weeks later there arrived a simple, almost primitive, painting of a bowl of flowers, exploding with colour. The shape was repeated underneath by a double shadow of the bowl, but shaped like two large church bells with clappers. The dynamic colour of the flowers and the joyous swing of the bells expressed a powerful sense of energy and release. With the picture came a letter. 'You have reached me, reached me, *the real me*; the soft, vulnerable me, the one that wants to climb out and flow, and be a kind and loveable person, instead of tautened up, spitting aggression. I was so HAPPY!' Since then, and obviously long past the six months, the paintings and the letters have continued.

The relationship of creativity to spirituality is something that is still, surprisingly, little understood, and is often dismissed as art therapy. By spirituality I mean the development of a person's innermost self, 'the real vulnerable me'. Sadly, as Joanna Trollope observes in her novel, *The Rector's Wife*, 'So many people lack the capacity to live life richly, at any level.' One is led therefore to ask the question: What is the purpose and the function of art? How does art affect the majority of people? Is it anything more than a luxury for a privileged few?

It is one of the functions of art to hold, as it were, the mirror up to nature, and by so doing to probe, question, challenge; which is why art can often be unsettling. Art sees beneath the surface. It is a graph of the human heart. As a boy, faced with Picasso's painting *A Woman in Grief*, I understood more clearly my own mother's grief when one day her face suddenly seemed to disintegrate before me. Picasso's portrait enabled me to see the face behind the known familiar face, the moment when my mother's ordinary maternal mask had slipped and I saw something of what lay behind – her fear, her helplessness. Today more than ever, at a time when 'the centre falls apart', there is a need for the arts as people cry out for meaning in their lives, for pattern and purpose, for shape and form. Because art is not dogma it does not offer certainties, but what it does do is speak of the mystery and wonder and pain in the universe. It is religious in the sense that all true art seeks to pierce the mystery of life, to create order out of chaos. Even when art seeks to portray chaos, darkness or evil, it does so in order that we may the better comprehend the chaos, darkness and evil within ourselves.

And in such a time as ours it is not enough for art to be fed passively to the spectator or listener. Of course there must be, and always will be, specialists, exponents of the highest quality, but we must realize also that the vast majority of people possess, no matter how unused, real creative and imaginative faculties. People today need to discover, or rediscover, how to give form to their most urgent feelings, conflicts, yearnings and joys, the 'real vulnerable me', so that they may the better understand themselves and others. Yet others may find the key to this world through the work described in this book, through ritual and, above all, the creation of new rituals. If rituals are to be meaningful today they have to be rethought and rediscovered for, like symbols, they become threadbare with use. As Jesus observed, you cannot put new wine into old bottles. To live our meaning is the spiritual task that Jung makes the very soul of his psychology.

Jung maintained that each of us begins with a blueprint for life. Each one of us has a unique destiny. But what counts is how we relate to that destiny. It is like being given a hand of playing cards. Some are given a good hand, with all the aces, and yet end up throwing away their chances, while there are others who start off with a poor hand but, by playing skilfully, end up winning the game. We each have a destiny but we are not predestined. It is our task to work with our individual destiny and yet, at the same time, allow life to shape and make us, for there are surprises in every game and we have to learn how to improvize, how to remain open to the unexpected and to absorb it into the final blueprint. We are what we have been but what we shall be is what we are now. Thus each moment is capable of redemption.

If we are to live our meaning, to sing our own song, tell our own tale, before we go hence, then we have to be prepared to go on a journey into the interior, in search of the riches that lie within each one of us. As all myths teach, it takes courage to plunge into the unknown, and on the way we must expect a series of trials or passages of the soul. A ritual is such a passage, and is rightly termed a rite of passage. The word 'passage' carries several meanings. It is a corridor or tunnel that links one place with another, and it also implies movement along such a space. Thus, in an initiation ritual the initiate will be moved from familiar to unfamiliar surroundings. The word 'passage' also suggests the passing of time, and in a sacred ritual we transcend time and, like Pericles in Shakespeare's play, are enabled to hear 'the music of the spheres'. We pass over from one state of being into another (just as in death we pass over from time into eternity), experiencing a *metanoia* or complete change. There is, at such a moment, an unalterable shift of perception. We can never again be what we once were. It is a process brought about not by intellectual debate, but by direct experience.

The definition of the word 'experience' is a key to the whole process. It means: to attempt, venture, or risk (the Greek *peira* is the source of our word 'empirical'). More directly it derives from the Latin *experientia* – denoting trial, proof, experiment – itself generated from *experiens*, the present participle of *experiri* to try, test. The suffixed, extended form of *per* is *peri-to*, from which comes *periculum* meaning trial, danger, peril. Experience is linked with risk rather than with cognitive learning. Thus the Greek verb means to 'pass through', hence the idea of experience as perilous passage. From *per* we also derive our words 'fare' and 'ferry'. In this way, as Victor Turner demonstrates in *From Ritual to Theatre*, 'We have in the word "experience" the cumulative ideas of a journey, a test, a ritual passage, an exposure to peril, a risk and a source of fear. By means of experience we fare fearfully through perils, taking experimental steps.'

By the word 'soul' I imply that which we sense to be the essential part of each one of us, the 'real vulnerable me', the spirit, soul, psyche. It is this essential part of us which all spiritual traditions teach survives death. It is our immortal part and separate from the shell of the body. Jane Gardam, the novelist, writing an obituary of Maggie Hemingway, a fellow writer, (*The Independent*, 17 May 1993) records: 'Maggie did not believe in death. She was a Buddhist and believed that the body must be left behind for the soul to progress. Her faith was entire and she "died" with great calmness and full of Grace.' The soul is the world within and it is to this inner world that ritual relates.

Each one of us is a pale reflection of our potential self. When Pindar advised, 'Become what thou art', he meant, as Dr Anthony Stevens has expressed it in *On Jung*, 'Abandon your superficial persona, your social clichés, your worldly habits, and discover the ideal human being latent in your soul, and befriend the personal daimon who lives there.' Joyce Grenfell once said, 'I think what I am doing is *losing* Joyce Grenfell and finding out the person God made. The older you get the more you realize that happiness is losing your false sense of what you are, your *false self*. What was that lovely quotation: Become what you are! Well, that interpreted means become what your true potential is, your spiritual wholeness.' As Socrates said, it is the unexamined, the unloved life that is not worth living.

There are various routes to the world within. For some it may be by way of analysis; for some by way of meditation and prayer. Yet rituals, like symbols, cannot be invented. They must well up from within, as dreams do. Some rituals will emerge from the vision of one individual who lives close to his or her own centre, as in the example of John Hencher's Easter ritual which was created by him for a small group of people for one particular occasion and never repeated; while others will emerge from within a whole group. Such rituals are, however, more than self-expression, which is in itself a limited exercise and one that all too often is merely narcissistic. All true ritual calls for discipline, patience, perseverance, leading to the discovery of the self within, the Tao, the God.

A great ritual, a fundamental myth is a door, and he who can experience the door within himself passes through it most intensely.

Peter Brook
There are no secrets

I

Exploration into Ritual

Carl Jung: Our personal psychology is finite, but what dwells within us has no boundaries, it surrounds us on all sides; it is fathomless as the deepest abyss; it is as vast as the sky.

Sigmund Freud: In that case it is no use to me. I am a psychologist not a mystic.

Carl Jung: But all authentic experience *is* mystical: the experience of Jesus, the Buddha, Mohammed, the seers and prophets of the Upanishads, the experience of the Eternal Ground at the very core of our soul. It is the mystery of being that lies beyond all sense and all thought that brings fulfilment, finality, absolute truth and lasting peace. *That* should be the goal of our psychology – not an endless groping after the squalid implications of infantile sexuality!

(From *Friends and Enemies*, a play by Anthony Stevens)

Ritual is one of the keys which can open a door into the realm of the imagination, that realm which is in fact the world of the collective unconscious. Beneath our conscious intelligence a deeper intelligence is at work, the evolving intelligence of mankind. We often say of someone who lacks imagination that they are to be pitied. To have imagination is to enjoy a richness of interior life, an uninterrupted flow of images. To have imagination is to see the world in its totality. Without imagination we are cut off from the deeper reality of life, from our souls. Jung regarded it as the task of modern man and woman to rediscover and reawaken those images that lie within us and which he termed the archetypes; to awaken them and contemplate them as they manifest themselves through dreams, visions and works of art. Each one of us has to discover our personal myth and learn to live by it. In certain dreams, as also in the exercises described in this book, key images will manifest themselves and these images serve as signposts on our life's journey. Even such a seemingly simple exercise as the *Scroll of Life* can have profound bearings upon the performer's life. As Mircea Eliade once observed, 'I believe that in such dreams one is being given an auto-revelation of one's own destiny. It is one's destiny that is revealed in the sense of an existence being directed towards a precise goal, an enterprise, a work that one ought to accomplish. It is a matter of your deep destiny, and therefore of the obstacles you are going to encounter, too; of serious, irreversible decisions you are going to have to make.'

Too many ancient rituals have lost contact with the deity. The virtual disappearance of rites of passage from our culture, together with a decline in the respect accorded to sacred ceremonial, has disconnected us from the archetypal imperatives which seek to transform our lives, and has left us without a mythic context to give them meaning. And yet, in his dreams, modern man continues to be pervaded by religious symbols, figures and themes. Religion has gone underground and lies buried in the deepest recesses of our psyches, waiting only, like Sleeping Beauty, to be reclaimed.

'The day one starts sensing the invisible dreams urging rocks, seeds, bodies and minds all around us on their predestined courses, the first step towards wisdom has been taken.' To achieve this we should meditate on those images which we carry within us for they are the maps by which we may chart the course of our individual journeys. If we can but give form to our feelings, define them rhythmically, dramatically, ritualistically; if we can fashion images of what it is we fear, desire, need, hunger for, aspire to, then that form will define the inner landscape and be made objective, so that we can visit it time and again, and begin to meditate upon those images and in this way grow. Individuation is about choosing one's own uniqueness, it involves not only self-realization but self-differentiation. To individuate, in the full Jungian meaning of the term, as Anthony Stevens explains, 'is to defy the tyranny of received opinion, to disengage from the banal symbols of mass culture and to confront the primordial symbols in the collective unconscious – in one's own unique way'.

Such rituals as are described here are like dreams and, like dreams, they continue to nourish and instruct us long afterwards. A dream has to be lived with. It is not a puzzle waiting to be solved by the intellect. It is, rather, a living reality and must be experienced. Certain key dreams, certain images, will last a lifetime. One such example is that of a young dancer in New York, Carolyn Gracey. She had been distressed by the death some months previously of a much loved teacher. How her ritual evolved over many weeks she herself describes: 'In working on my individual piece I learned through experience that we cannot work on a subject unless we can look at it objectively. This I found out when doing my solo on Mr B's death. The ritual which followed was the result of my being deeply disturbed by a class discussion in which several of my fellow students attacked the idea of the existence of God. I was so upset by this that I spent a tortured night, unable to sleep. The following day when I met with James in the studio I was so uptight that when he asked me to relax and just let something come, I became even more tense until suddenly the conflict and trouble in my mind spilled over into the improvisation out of which the final ritual evolved.'

Carolyn's first attempts before this had been either sentimental or melodramatic, more like psycho-drama, being too preoccupied with her own feeling response to her bereavement. The class discussion served to help her face the central issue: what is beyond death? As a result her unconscious began to work, releasing in the improvisation those essential images she needed. Carolyn called her piece *From Forth This Circle* and it remains for me one of the most vivid examples of a personal ritual that I have experienced. She began, seated on the floor, inside a child's wooden hoop, rocking backwards and forwards in an agitated manner, muttering a repetitive sound which eventually articulated itself as the words 'No God!' This phrase she repeated over and over, monotonously: 'No God, No God, No God, No God, No God!' She began to wrestle with the hoop, rising up with it, as though she were trapped inside it, at the bottom of a deep well. Repeatedly she cried out the words of her private terror until, at the climax, she gave a cry of despair and collapsed to the ground, the wooden hoop rattling around her until, finally, it lay silent.

She remained quite still. In the silence a flute was heard playing. Slowly opening her eyes, she gazed at the wooden circle inside which she was sitting, as though now seeing it from a different perspective, as though inside the terror lay the answer. Reaching out her hands she fingered the hoop gently, tenderly, and then began to sing, like a child singing a nursery rhyme, the words 'My circle is my God. My God is my circle.' Lifting the hoop, she stood up, holding it high above her head like a spinning halo of light. Gazing up into it she sang out with intense joy the words of her revelation: '*My circle encompasses me!*'

That was all, but the simplicity of this short work, the intensity of its emotion, its crystallization of a real and recognizable human dilemma, recalled some of those delicate and fragmentary poems of Emily Dickinson, each one a minute but precise graph of a mood and of her own spiritual development.

> I never saw a Moor –
> I never saw the Sea –
> Yet know I how the Heather looks
> And what a billow be.
> I never spoke with God
> Nor visited in Heaven –
> Yet certain am I of the spot
> As if the Checks were given.

By means of this ritual Carolyn was enabled to move from a personal to a transpersonal plane, and to commence her own journey towards individuation, as is plain from her discovery of her own mandala, that age-old symbol of wholeness and totality, circular in form, with the emphasis upon the centre and usually containing some reference to the deity.

Ritual takes many forms. At the simplest level there are those recurring personal rituals which we all use for getting up in the morning, going off to work, settling down to work, coming home, relaxing, going to bed. All such personal rituals enable us to come to terms with the reality of each day, imposing some kind of order on what otherwise might be chaos. There are rituals relating to every aspect of life: rituals of dress, which is to do with our identity and the way in which we do or do not reveal ourselves to others; of courting, of sexuality, of the office or workplace, of school, of the armed services or other organizations. More complex rituals have evolved for the family, clan, tribe or nation, while the classic rituals all place the individual in a larger context so that birth, puberty, marriage and death are seen as timeless experiences which have occurred to generations of individuals. Such rituals validate, providing an image of forces controlling life, and serving to reinforce our ability to cope with an unpredictable world. They heighten the intensity of shared experience, enabling us to realize that we are not alone but part of an indivisible whole. And while it has been customary to describe many seasonal festivals as attempts to control nature, the dominant note in all truly religious ceremonial is that of submission to the inevitability of destiny. No rite has yet succeeded in keeping winter at bay any more than King Canute could hold back the waves by commanding them to stand still; nor can rites of spring guarantee an abundant harvest. Such rituals serve rather to help us to accept the rhythms of the seasons: of seed-time and harvest; of spring-time and winter; of birth and death; all culminating in those rites of a dying and a resurrecting God.

The greatest of all rituals are, of course, religious. Religion, being a search for meaning in the universe, offers a series of rituals to mark the seasons and events in the life of an individual or of a nation. As Joseph Campbell said of the state funeral of President Kennedy: 'The nation was unstrung. The archetypal event of his funeral allowed us to meditate on death and the mystery of death as epitomized in the highest presence in our national life. There were six horses, as I remember, and the seventh had its rider and stirrups reversed, a rite that goes back to the ancient Aryans. Out of it came a sense of resolution for the country.'

All true rituals mark a transition from one mode of being to another, working a transformation within the individual or community, at a deep psychological, physical and spiritual level, resulting in an altered state of consciousness. Such major rituals, as we have seen, are sometimes known as rites of passage. Clearly the passage is not geographical, from point A to point B, but rather a journey of the heart, into the interior landscape of each individual, resulting in 'a sea-change into something rich and strange', as Shakespeare wrote in *The Tempest*. I have often wondered whether the writing of that play was for Shakespeare a rite of passage into age and the acceptance of the diminishing of his own powers. I now find this echoed by Helen Luke in *Old Age – Journey into Simplicity*, in which she writes, 'Shakespeare in *The Tempest*, his last great play, has left us images of a *rite de passage* that may arouse questions and awaken intuitions of meaning hidden in the years already lived in time, and they point forward to the changes of attitude which must come to us if we are to seek a deeper and more conscious approach to death in our later years. *The Tempest* is above all a play about transformations. King Alonso, Ferdinand, Miranda, Caliban – all of these change in the play; but these changes are a kind of expansion, a consequence of the ageing Prospero himself as he approaches the moment when he will set Ariel free.'

All rites of passage, as Arnold van Gennep observed in his classic study, *Rites of Passage*, involve three stages. The first is a ritual of separation, involving washings and purifications, aimed at separating the individual from his former life. This is followed by the central stage during which the initiate may be hidden, buried, stripped naked, or exposed to danger or to the elements. Among the Hopi Indians the boy is taken into the *kiva*, an under-ground womb-like cave, while in the rite of Attis the initiate would be stripped naked and, after a period of fasting, lowered into a pit and the blood of a newly slain bull poured over him. On emerging, covered with blood, like a baby from its mother's womb, he would be fed, like a baby, for several days, entirely on milk.

During his various trials the initiate is stripped of all familiar associations, and is inducted into the spiritual context of his tribe or clan. Often he is wounded: a tooth is knocked out by one of the elders, or an incision made on some part of his body. Such an act is not performed sadistically but reverberates out of a rich centre of meaning. This central part of the initiation may last weeks or months, during which the boy is kept apart from the rest of the community. Van Gennep has named this the liminal state, drawing upon the Latin word *limen*, meaning threshold. The initiate crosses over the threshold from one stage of life to another, and once he has crossed he can never return. The concluding stage of such an initiation ritual is one of incorporation, enabling the individual to re-enter society on a new basis.

'The significance of ritual is that it constellates a profound *experience*, it provides a traditionally sanctified opportunity to accomplish a *transformation of the ego's experience of the Self* ... Now I am a boy belonging to my mother – Now I am a boy leaving my mother and submitting myself to the ritual that the gods have decreed – Now I die as a boy and am ritually dismembered – Now I am born as a man among men.' It is interesting to note that at the age of eight a Brahmin boy will enact a ritual called *Going on a pilgrimage to Benares*, in the course of which, and for the last time in his life, he shares food with his mother. Thereafter he is given an adult's white loin cloth. I recall also an Indian student of mine who is a Zoroastrian priest (he was ordained when he was about nine years old), describing how the family guru would visit his mother at intervals and say to her, 'Give me what you value most.' She would give him a ruby necklace, or a gold bracelet, until one day he came and asked her to hand over her son. Today in the West we have no such rituals. Robert Bly, in his inspirational book, *Iron John*, discusses the lack of such rituals for the young. 'The recovery of some form of initiation,' he writes, 'is essential for the culture.'

Time and again we lack rituals which can mark and celebrate such essential rites of passage. As Harvey Cox has written, 'I believe that as a culture we are ritually out of phase. We are dragooned into rituals that mean little or nothing to us – saluting flags, national anthems, Cómmencements, even bar mitzvahs and confirmations – yet when we need the symbolic deepening of an important experience we somehow lack the necessary gestures and images.' He describes his own baptism, one of total immersion, at the age of ten, before he was ready for it, but was given no ritual with which to confront and mark his subsequent adolescence. 'Today in America we have few, if any, puberty rites. Children pass awkwardly and without ritual through sprouting pubic hair,

menstruation, changing voice, having wet dreams, getting hold of
the family car keys. No wonder we undergo identity crises until we
die. Rituals should mark and celebrate the transition from one
phase of life to the next.' Similarly Mircea Eliade in conversation
with Claude-Henri Rocquet responded to the question 'How are
we to tell our children that they are sexual and mortal beings?' as
follows: 'Today not only has sexuality been desacralised, but
death has too; it is ignored. The sight and thought of it are
repressed. In a profane society it is very difficult to initiate children
into these two great mysteries. I have no answer. Is it actually
possible for a child to understand death or sexuality? I don't know
what one ought to say.'

It is not only sex and death, however, that today lack rituals, but
many other transitions in life. Rosemary Manning, in her novel,
The Open Door has a character observe, 'Oh, God, why is there
no satisfactory ritual for *parting*? The pain is raw at the edges: no
healing balm of sherry.' Today we have no rituals for a woman
who has been raped, beaten or battered; no rituals for parents who
have had to experience an abortion, a miscarriage or, even worse,
a still-born baby. There are no rituals for pregnancy; none for a
broken marriage, a broken relationship or a broken home. What
rituals do we have for a child moving to a new school or a new
neighbourhood, or a young person going off to her first job? What
rituals exist for a young woman's first menstruation? What rituals
for a boy coming to puberty? What rituals exist for the ongoing
experience of marriage? We have none comparable to the orthodox Jewish practice of the mikvah bath.

This ritual bath for women is not about physical cleansing since
she must already have showered or bathed before entering. Its
purpose is of a much higher order. It serves as a means of protecting the woman's individuality. She has time to think and be by
herself. For a few days each month the woman withdraws into her
femaleness and the man into his maleness, and then once again they
come together as man and wife. A re-evaluation and a renewal of
the marriage takes place, allowing the relationship to develop on
many different levels. It is a ritual which recalls those words of the
Prophet on marriage: 'Let there be spaces in your togetherness.'

What rituals exist for the elders of our society, be they the wise women and men in our midst, or those fragile victims of senility or Alzheimer's whom we must support? Why do we so often wait until someone is dead before we say how much we valued them? We have need of rituals for ageing, as each of us grows into old age and moves towards our eventual departure. And while each of the major faiths has precise rituals for the dying and the dead, what rituals do we have to offer to those of no specific faith or tradition? As May Sarton writes in her novel, *As We Are Now* 'What rite of passage is there for the dying, especially where there is no faith in God?' And even among existing religious institutions which have their own ancient liturgies there is often felt the need for alternative forms. A nun, having read my book, *Inner Journey, Outer Journey* wrote, 'I'm especially interested in and inspired by your exploration of drama spilling over into liturgy, creating our own liturgies that are relevant to us today – *and all this rooted and fed from our deepest centre.*'

A ritual is not to be confused with ceremonial, although ceremonial is a part of ritual. Ceremonial is concerned with the externals, varying arrangements of text, flowers, movement and music. New rituals, if they are to be efficacious, must well up from within the psyche of the individual or of a group. I have found, as have others working in this field, that when people are given the opportunity and the responsibility of creating their own rituals the results are often unexpected and surprising. For there is among people today a real hunger for the things of the spirit and, in many, a deep need to rediscover within themselves a sense of the *noumenos*, of the sacred, an encounter with that which gives meaning to their lives. Ritual works on two levels, that of the psychological and that of the spiritual, and sometimes both coincide. A ritual can resolve, at a deeper level than the intellect, some inner conflict, thereby releasing the individual from a psychological block. Bani Shorter, in her book on women's initiations, *An Image Darkly Forming* observes, 'Ritual is a collective or individual attempt to conjure up or reawaken those deeper layers of the psyche which the light of reason and the power of the will can never reach, and to bring them back to life.' I recall a letter I once received from a woman who had done seven years of intensive in-depth work as a psychotherapist, in which she wrote,

Like most psychotherapies my training has been mainly a conscious, verbal process, and a very effective one. It has given me invaluable help in my own journey, and has been a very humanizing influence on my Catholic spirituality. However, I am at the limit of what I can do consciously and verbally and my personal process is no longer about personality work. I have been aware for quite a while that in spite of the very good therapy I have had there is still something very deep inside me that is still wounded and controls most of my responses to the world; that in spite of the depth and breadth of my spiritual understanding and love of God, somewhere inside me I am still a prisoner. Somewhere I *don't* know myself. There are doors inside me that are shut and I want to open them or, at least, have the opportunity of opening them or not, as is appropriate. I stand baffled and bewildered at my own boundaries, not knowing how or where to cross, and everything, every good thing, I have learned and believed up to now, being no longer sufficient to see me through, *I need a new knowing.*

A ritual is a journey of the heart which should lead us into the inner realm of the psyche and, ultimately, into that of the soul, what Meister Eckhart referred to as 'the ground of our being'. Rituals, if performed with passion and devotion, will enhance our desire and strengthen our capacity to live. New rituals will evolve but the ancient rituals and liturgies are also capable of rediscovery as we learn to make them our own. Among many Christians the sign of the cross has become a perfunctory gesture, even verging on mindless superstition. And yet, if we open ourselves to its deeper meaning it can, once again, come alive, and be seen not only as the central symbol of Christianity but a profound archetype for everyone, for this crossroads sign, this meeting-of-the-opposites, is to be found in many cultures and throughout history.

In order to rediscover the sign of the cross as a meaningful ritual it is necessary first of all to centre down, allowing all thoughts to settle. There are many ways of doing this but perhaps the simplest is by following the breath as it comes in and goes out, and resting in the emptiness after the breath has been expelled. In its own rhythm the breath will flow back, filling the lungs, and again it will expel itself. All we have to focus on is breathing in, breathing out, and resting in the moments of non-breath. We allow ourselves to be breathed in and breathed out. When thoughts come to distract us we gently let them go, and return to concentrating on the breath. Once we are truly centred then we can begin to explore the sign of the cross.

Traditionally the right hand goes to the forehead on the words 'In the name of the Father'. In the centre of the forehead is the chakra known as the third eye. It is through this chakra that spiritual enlightenment enters. It is interesting that in the famous portrait of St Dominic, the founder of the Church's intellectual order, he is portrayed with a star shining just above his forehead. If now we reach up higher with the right hand, above the head, we have a sense of the Father as Abba (meaning 'the origin of all things') descending from on high and entering into us. With this gesture we draw down power from on high, God coming down to earth and becoming human.

And now, on the words 'and of the Son', the hand descends to the level of the heart chakra which for the Hindu is the centre of *bhakti* (devotion). 'The real place of the Divine Encounter,' writes Abhishiktananda, 'is in the very centre of our being, the place of our origin, from which all that we are is constantly welling up. Thus to direct the attention towards the heart, even in a physical way, is symbolically to turn all activities towards the very centre of ourselves.' India, he remarks, has from the beginning been alive to the mystery of the heart, the *guha*, the 'cave' within, as it is called in her scriptures, the abode of Brahman, the very place of Atman itself, the truest self of man. It is the source of everything.

And so the hand rests at the heart, knowing that the word is made flesh in each of us, for 'the kingdom of heaven is within'. The inner world, as Carl Jung taught, is just as real as the outside world; in fact it is more real for it is infinite and everlasting and does not change or decay as the outside world constantly does. It was Jung's achievement to discover the empirical existence not only of the personal unconscious, of which both Freud and Adler had also been aware, but of the collective unconscious behind it, with its archetypes and infinite possibilities.

When we are ready (and all this should take its own time) the right hand and the left hand should move outwards on each side of the body on the words 'and of the Holy Spirit', so that the arms are outspread like the wings of a bird, an image of the spirit brooding upon the waters of chaos before the creation of the world. Thus extended, the arms are like a gesture of embrace, of compassion for the entire world. Then, slowly, the arms begin to close in to encircle one's own self, nurturing the Christ (or the Buddha) within. We reach out and then we draw in. After a while we release the arms and go out to the world, releasing the peace, the joy and the strength that is found in the cave of the heart. Reaching out and drawing in, breathing in and breathing out.

There is something else to be discovered about the sign of the cross. It is a sign, and to cross is to signify. Those who cannot write their own names are asked to sign with a cross. It is the primordial signature, as Bani Shorter observes in her paper, *If Ritual Dies*. 'Crossings and cross-roads are of deep symbolic meaning in life. It was Hermes, the Messenger of the Gods, who was guardian of the cross-roads in ancient Greece. There, where one is challenged by change of direction and choice, one encounters one's god, and signifies as oneself and to oneself but also in relation to that Other.'

As we reach up and draw down into ourselves the strength and power of the divine, so this movement descends on a vertical line, plunging into the centre of our being, and dissecting the horizontal line of the final gesture. The vertical line of God and infinity cuts through the horizontal line of mankind and time, creating a tension of opposites. And it is at the centre of this tension that each of us has to learn how to live, uniting in each of us all opposites: male/female, dark/light, reason/intuition, God/humans, sacred/secular. 'The one hope for our torn world,' writes Barbara Hannah in *Encounters with the Soul*, 'is that the warring opposites should meet. This was the main endeavour of alchemy. The alchemists were always trying to marry the opposites to each other, for it is only when opposites are united that true peace is to be found. Collectively we cannot do anything for, as Jung constantly said, the only place we can do anything is in the individual, in ourselves. If we are in Tao – that place where all opposites are united – we have an inexplicable effect upon our surroundings.' We cannot be freed permanently of the warring opposites in this life but we can realize that there is a place in us where they are united, and we can learn to visit it, as Carolyn Gracey did in the ritual described in the Introduction. If enough individuals realize this, says Barbara Hannah, and go to this inner place, they will be able to stand the tension of the opposites outside.

Every symbol may lose its *mana*. Sometimes the symbol is simply worn out, used up, exhausted; and where this is the case then a new symbol must be born in that person; or it may be that the individual has to rediscover the life within the archetype. We need also to remember that just because a particular ritual or liturgy no longer works for us, that is not to say that it no longer has any validity. For someone else it may well be the way into the inner wellsprings of being. The way in which new symbols manifest themselves and new rituals evolve, and new life is discovered within ancient symbols, is the subject of this book.

II

Journeying to the Frontier

'I stand baffled and bewildered at my own boundaries not knowing how or where to cross.'

A ritual may involve an actual journey (pilgrimage) of short or long duration. It may take the pilgrim simply around a church or temple or it may cover thousands of miles, taking him or her to a famous shrine or holy place – Mecca, the Holy Land, Benares, the River Ganges, Lourdes, Lough Derg, etc. A pilgrim proceeds to a faraway place in search of a shared adventure and returns finally 'to a renewed home space. In short, he is *en route* to his roots.' The journey may be not to a famous shrine but to a place rich in personal association to the individual. Bani Shorter describes such a journey, which is a striking example of a personal ritual created out of an inner necessity at a particular time and place. Nicole was a musician, married to a musician, and together they created a dream house. Suddenly she felt a shadow fall over her marriage, her future and her career. She found that she could not 'lift a finger to her instrument', and since she was not only a gifted but also an acclaimed musician this led her into analysis. Slowly she came to accept the break-up of the marriage, found somewhere else to live, and began the divorce settlements. The major emotional hurdle, however, was having to move out of her dream house. Then one day she cancelled her appointment with her analyst. Instead she went back to the now empty house (her former husband was away on a concert tour). It took her three days to complete what she had set out to do. She cleaned the place from top to bottom, mowed the lawn, pruned the hedge and weeded the garden. She cried a lot, but she forced herself to sleep in the house alone each night.

> When her task had been completed at last, on the evening of the third day, she had gone out and gathered flowers from the garden, brought them in and arranged them in all her favourite places. The house was beautiful, she said. She had then bathed and dressed and packed her bag. But, before she had left, during the long twilight of the still evening, she had drawn her instrument from the case, lifted her fingers and played a recital of favourite pieces. When she closed the door at last, she put her key through the letter-box, leaving the home-no-longer-hers behind forever.

She had, as Bani Shorter says, 'conducted a funeral rite for the death of a romantic childhood fantasy and, in so doing, had reached a new stage of life.'

One of the exercises which I use regularly in my workshops and which can become a very powerful rite of passage takes the image of a journey to a frontier. We begin with the word itself: 'frontier'. What is a frontier? What happens at a frontier? It is a barrier, a boundary, a division, a crossing line, a threshold, at which we are asked to declare our identity, show a passport, provide the correct password, declare our intention: are we friend or enemy? At the frontier we are betwixt and between, standing between past and future, in limbo. And then what lies beyond the frontier? It may be the North or South Pole; Eldorado; the Land of the Setting, or Rising, Sun; Paradise; Nirvana; King Arthur's Avalon 'where I will heal me of my grievous wound'. Or it may be a place of terror: purgatory, hell, Hades – like Jean-Paul Sartre's *Huis-Close*, a place of no return. Beyond the frontier may be swamps, sinking sands, minefields, the enemy. It may be an ocean, recalling Emily Dickinson's 'Exultation is the going of an inland soul to sea!'; it may be a forest or a jungle or the desert where Jesus was tempted by the devil, alone with wild beasts, (both aspects of his *shadow* side) and comforted by angels. The Japanese actor, Yoshi Oida, who has worked with Peter Brook for the past twenty years, describes how at the end of their long and hot journey through Africa, 'All you had left was yourself, who had journeyed for one hundred days through various places and experiences. There was nothing you could do except re-examine that self. In the end, there is only yourself, nothing else. This is the mystery.'

The frontier will have all sorts of associations according to the individual doing the exercise. It may stand for the frontier between childhood and adolescence, innocence and experience, virgin and woman, boy and man. It may remind us of specific, autobiographical frontiers between people: parents and children, teachers and pupils, Protestants and Catholics, Muslims and Hindus, the North and the South, 'them' and 'us'. We may be reminded of the frontier as it appears in mythology, fairy tale and folklore: of Alice journeying through the frontier of the Looking Glass into the world of the imagination (that same world which in C.S. Lewis's Narnia books is entered through a wardrobe). Similarly Orphé in Jean Cocteau's film enters the underworld through a mirror, while in the classical legend Orpheus has to cross the River Styx and confront the dog Cerberus if he is to rescue Eurydice. When we arrive at the frontier we may be reminded of the opening lines from Shakespeare's *Hamlet*: 'Nay, stand and unfold yourself!' Indeed, a rite of passage is a challenge to our true identity, and may call for a discarding of our present identity. It is significant how frequently in dreams there appears the image of the dreamer being without a passport or any means of identification. In the last analysis few of us really know ourselves, and who we are. In Tennessee Williams's play *Camino Real*, La Dame Aux Camélias breaks down when she cannot find her papers, and the plane which would have rescued her has to leave without her.

The word 'frontier' contains within it two words: 'front', and 'tier'. The word front implies a façade, or being in the foreground, as in the expression 'up front'; while in the First World War the expression 'the front line' indicated the place of greatest danger. The word tier indicates layers or terraces, so that on arrival at the frontier we may well discover that there is not one but many frontiers, one behind the other. Often in life we think we have broken through one problem only to find that there is another and another, each waiting to be solved, like a series of tests, or trials, awaiting a Ulysses.

When we arrive at the frontier we may find that it has changed. What may have appeared as some distant Eldorado when first we set out may be found to have become an impenetrable wall of stone, of iron, or of fire. We may feel challenged to leap through the fire, risking the danger. Or the frontier may appear to us like a river or a flowing stream, into which we lower the wounded foot; suddenly it is healed and we are able to stride forward into the new world that awaits us. We may hurl ourselves against the impenetrable wall and discover it is electrocuted, and so collapse. Such an image may well be telling us that it is foolish to proceed any further, that now is not the time for such a transition. We may find that we are compelled to return to base and await another day, or else to remain patiently at the frontier until the situation changes.

Often when doing this exercise the individual is reminded of the oracular wisdom of *The Book of Changes*. The possibilities are endless, and for each person the journey is always different. For some it may be a journey into the world of the imagination, while to some it may become a true rite of passage, as happened to each of the following, who were students at an American college where I was teaching a course on ritual. Each exemplifies the words of Bani Shorter, 'Though I can plan to make a pilgrimage, which is a rite projected in space, I cannot plan for what the pilgrimage will make of me.' Both students were in their early twenties.

FROM MONICA'S JOURNAL

As I was meditating at the start, gazing at the frontier, the impulse that hit me all of a sudden was my sexuality, my virginity. At first I was happy to advance towards the frontier because it was far away. I saw myself falling for a guy and this expressed itself in the form of a somersault. Then curiosity and crawling along the ground took me a little closer, but I was still comfortably far enough away from the big decision. I was learning and growing in my knowledge, which was a good thing. This feeling slowly changed as I started to feel a pressure pushing me towards the frontier, as if this guy were pressurizing me more and more. When I realized that I was really in love with him I expressed this feeling by a head-over-heels cartwheel. However this also brought me closer to the frontier. I began to feel alarmed at being so close to this barrier and now I began to look backwards, not wanting to face what lay ahead. I was still curious about the dangerous frontier and so, in order to get closer, I lay on my back with my head facing towards the frontier and, in this position, stretched out my arms until my finger tips touched the frontier itself. At this moment I experienced an instant revulsion and my whole body shrank away. I felt torn between staying where I was and exploring further. So I lay on my stomach for a long while, contemplating the frontier. Then finally I advanced towards it. Being this close to it and actually *seeing* it kind of shook me up, and so I curled up into a ball in order to protect myself from the intense pressure I was feeling and the responsibility of making a decision. I knew I couldn't stay in this position for ever, so I stretched out my body lengthwise so that I lay now alongside the frontier, and I waited for the big decision to occur. After nearly rolling over the frontier, tensed and wavering, I finally rolled right back to where I had started – and so remained a virgin.

This whole experience was very intense for me and I think it represents a major conflict I have with college. The guys here seem only interested in one-night stands which I have no desire to get caught up in. Yet the only alternative is to be ignored, to be left out – which results in my very strong anti-male feelings and my being uncomfortable around guys. There is a lot of pressure to go with the crowd and as I am a virgin I am in a very small minority for students these days. Sometimes I question myself but this exercise has really helped me to realize that I'm not ready for sex and that I am strong enough to stand up for my own convictions. It means being lonely now but I know I feel better about myself for it. I hold the controlling hand.

Monica's account illustrates the pressure put upon young women, especially in Western society, to lose their virginity, a pressure which is far greater than many people wish to acknowledge. Sandra

Berwick, writing in *The Independent* (27 March 1993) describes the case of Ceri Evans, aged 17, and her son Nicky, aged 3. She was twelve years old when she fell in love with an older, more sophisticated man – of sixteen. Even at the age of twelve, re- marked Ceri, there was strong pressure from her peer group to have sexual intercourse. 'From everyone, boys and girls. I resisted for eight months. But you feel like the wimp of the group if you don't. I got sick of the pressure all the time.' As she sums up, 'I knew all about condoms, but nothing of love.' Sally Cline, in her book *Women, Celibacy and Passion*, quotes Sandy, a nineteen- year-old Canadian, recalling how:

> In our class, around thirteen or fourteen, there was terrible pressure on us to lose our virginity. Some of us didn't want to. We were kinda young, I guess; there wasn't a real specific reason, other than some of the guys being pushy. But we didn't stand much of a chance. I went around in a gang. We were close buddies, but the guys hated us ganging up and not caring what they thought. So they just made it impossible for us to stick together. They wanted us to lose it; it was push, push all the time. It was kinda heavy. Your virginity got to be a goddam handicap so you had to give in and lose it.

Monica's ability to resist the pressure to go with the crowd, to compete with her peers, to refuse to yield to male expectations and, instead, to be her own person, recalls a poem by Emily Dickinson (who similarly stood her own ground): 'I'm ceded – I've stopped being Theirs.' Monica's journey also reminded me of Martha Graham's theatre-ritual *Errand into the Maze*, in which Ariadne enters the maze in order to confront the minotaur. At first she dare not look at the minotaur (portrayed by a male dancer) but, at the climax, she dares to look him in the face and it is at this moment that she ceases to be afraid and, climbing onto his back, rides him triumphantly out of the maze. Like Prospero who, at the end of *The Tempest*, is able to say of Caliban, the monster, 'This thing of darkness I acknowledge as my own', so Graham was acting out ritualistically the purgation of our own darkness and the revelation of our innermost selves. It was theatre at its deepest level.

The second illustration comes from another student at the same college. He was a philosophy student, very well read, articulate, but had never done anything like this before and his journal records how he was often 'pissed off' by the exercises. But he persevered. He tried the Frontier exercise more than once but got nowhere with it. 'The motions felt contrived,' he wrote, 'and the images were forced. Nothing really flowed.' Then suddenly he changed his strategy.

FROM DICKSON'S JOURNAL

Concentrating from the beginning, I developed a central image before I even made the first movement. In my mind I pictured a girl, a Colorado student, whom I have observed from a distance but with whom I have never actually talked. She is quite beautiful and her beauty often captivates my imagination. I pictured her as I know her – from a distance. As I moved forward, crawling first on my belly, then on my hands and knees, and finally walking up-right, so, gradually, I drew nearer to her. My images changed from a distant picture of her alone to close-ups of her and me together. The images luckily weren't limited to sexual pictures. I often found myself moving in an active daydream of a long life with this girl, of love, of true love, and the full range of activities that love consists of. I learned of the benefits and the commitment needed. I learned of the need and the desires of both her and me. The images of the two of us were closest and clearest after I first stood up, about halfway through the exercise. Then they grew distant and dull. In the end I found myself lying on the frontier without crossing over.

The frontier was the passage from life into death. The journey began, as it should, from my present state of mind. The journey focused on a love affair that lasted the rest of my life. It was a love that enabled me to beat the loneliness of death. With love I lost the existential hunger that constantly spears me at this stage of my life. I found a fuller sense of life that filled in the black hole of expecta-tion of death that plagues the hungry human. I don't think that I could have lived this love had it not been for the exercise. I merely would have remained contented with the sexual fantasies of my daydream. I don't know if the feeling and understanding spanned by the ritual will remain or if it will subside as actual love subsides, but I know that today I experienced love and can enjoy it, at least for a day.

Mircea Eliade, Harvey Cox, Robert Bly, Robert Moore and many others have commented upon the lack of rituals in our society which could enable the young to come to terms with their sexuality. The churches cannot help them because Christian teaching has yet to come to terms with the central drive of the sexual libido and to evolve a theology of sexuality. Yet it is clear from the accounts of both Monica and Dickson that such an exercise as described, when impelled by the urgency of the need within, is capable of becoming a true rite of passage, enabling each to emerge from their own labyrinth.

'Somewhere I don't know myself!' is a cry from the heart which we can all recognize; and each one of us, deep down, would respond to the following words, which were almost the last that Katherine Mansfield wrote in her journal, a few days before her death. 'I want to be all that I am capable of becoming — to be rooted in life — to learn, desire to know, to feel, to think, to act . . . We all fear when we are in waiting-rooms. Yet we must pass beyond them.' Ritual, at such a level, is a way of revitalizing, of providing a vision for life, whether for an individual, for a community or for a nation. In many studies of ritual it is claimed that repetition is an essential ingredient, but this is not necessarily so. The experiences of Monica, of Dickson and of Nicole (as cited by Bani Shorter) show clearly that a ritual which has evolved from a particular need does not necessarily have to be repeated. Once created and performed, it lives on in the psyche of the individual, continuing to work at an unconscious level. The images that arise from these depths should be meditated upon, just as one continues to meditate upon the images of certain dreams, not trying to resolve them at an intellectual level, but living with them, and slowly absorbing their meaning.

Ritual uses many forms of art but it is essentially, as Victor Turner observed, performance, enactment. Its performance quality differs, however, from theatre as we know it in the West, in that what is created is performed out of necessity. As such it is essential to the life-being of the individual. To the extent that it results in a deeper integration of the individual performing it, so it will affect the community in which that individual lives and works. What is certain is that, in a world which is increasingly fragmented, and in a radical process of change, new rituals will emerge, born out of such necessity.

III

Going on Pilgrimage

'Proclaim the pilgrimage among men,' the Koran proclaimed 1400 years ago. 'They will come to thee on foot and mounted on every kind of camel, lean on account of journeys through deep and distant mountains.'

Pilgrimage, especially as a penitential activity, is an ancient form of worship which may be described as a ritual on the move, and which continues to this day among all the major faiths. Each year some four million Catholics journey to Lourdes, while more than ten million Indians make their way to bathe in the River Ganges. Ahmed Rashid, writing in *The Independent* on 26 June 1991, recorded how 'in appalling heat and in a landscape of utter desolation, nearly two million pilgrims achieved the zenith of their spiritual life last Friday when they stood and prayed on the Plain of Arafat, ten miles north of Mecca ... Muslims, following rituals set out first by the Prophet Abraham and then by the Prophet Mohammed, gather here to ask God's forgiveness for their sins.'

Pilgrims, whatever their religious tradition, are engaged in a search for meaning and for spiritual advancement. A pilgrimage dramatizes the quest for the divine, but, as Tara Tulku Rimpoche has written, there are various levels of pilgrimage, relating to the motivation involved. There are those who go on a pilgrimage solely to get merit for themselves, and those who go not only for themselves but 'simultaneously wish all beings to go with them. In a sense they visualize that they are taking all beings with them on the pilgrimage ... and that becomes a vast root of virtue.'

Until the nineteenth century, Muslim pilgrims setting out from

Cairo, Baghdad, from Morocco or the Sudan, from Samarkand or Sumatra, would face sandstorms and shortages of water, and be in danger from marauding tribes. Similarly, Christian pilgrims would be drowned at sea, or their ships attacked by pirates. To travel to Rome from northern Europe meant crossing the Alps which were especially hazardous in winter. Many died on the way from sickness or exhaustion, while others added to their hardships by fasting, wearing a hairshirt or binding penitential chains about their near-naked bodies. It is no wonder that, before setting forth, pilgrims were encouraged to make their wills, and that a service of dedication would be held in which the pilgrims were blessed and such resounding prayers as the following pronounced over them:

> O God, who required Abraham to leave his country and preserved him safe and sound throughout his travels, grant to your children the same protection; uphold us in perils and lighten our journey; be unto us a shade against the sun, a covering against the rain and the cold, support us in our weariness and defend us against every danger; be unto us a staff to prevent falling and a port to welcome the shipwrecked; so that, guided by You, we may attain our goal with certitude and may return home safe and sound. Amen.

But, one must ask, does the modern pilgrimage, made more comfortable by modern travel, carry the same penitential meaning? The purpose of such a pilgrimage is surely to summon us away from the safe and familiar pattern of every day into 'a context of danger and distance and demand'. It is here that Eamon Duffy, writing in *The Tablet*, suggests that Irish-style pilgrimage (and to that I would add Polish) has a distinctive contribution to make 'which more gentle – I almost wrote genteel – shrines like Walsingham with its neat lawns and its tea room, seem to me to lack. In the raw experience of hunger, cold, lack of sleep, and the elemental contact with earth, rock and water, unshielded by roof or shoe leather, we can find a sense of fragility and creatureliness which is vital to any true perception of our humanity, and of the majesty and permanence of God.'

He describes a personal pilgrimage, undertaken in 1989, which he made to Skellig Michael, one of the great Irish holy places. An early Christian monastery perched on a pinnacle of stone 8 miles out in the Atlantic, off the coast of Kerry, it remained until the last century a place of penitential pilgrimage, and was both arduous and dangerous: drownings were not uncommon, and once on the island the pilgrim had a hair-raising climb to the monastery and was expected to inch out on a rock spar reaching into the void, to kiss a cross carved at the end. On the day that Eamon Duffy went, a force 9 gale developed while their small wooden boat was at sea. They landed with difficulty and by the time they left there was a 12-foot swell at the jetty, and they had to leap for the deck as it roared past. 'The journey there and back in what seemed mountainous seas was one of the most chastening, but also one of the most liberating, experiences of my life. The comforts of modern tourism were briefly torn away, to be replaced by an elemental confrontation with one's own frailty and mortality, one of the essential purposes of pilgrimage.'

With the exception of a modern site such as Knock, which is more like a hypermarket of piety, the shrines of Ireland – Lough Derg, Croagh Patrick, Our Lady's Island – all involve a similar discomfort as the pilgrims kneel on cold wet stones, walk barefoot over sharp scree, or wade through icy water. The Lough Derg pilgrimage lasts for three days, during which pilgrims are required to abstain from all food and drink except the black tea and dry toast served just twice, while no sleep is allowed for two days and a night. Twenty thousand people a year submit to a gruelling regime of fasting, sleeplessness and physical devotions, while over 25,000 every year, many of them barefoot, make the arduous climb to the summit of Croagh Patrick.

Similar pilgrimages, some of them centuries old, continue to this day in Poland. Some of them last as long as a week and draw people from hundreds of miles away, many of them journeying on foot, as China Galland describes in her book, *Longing for Darkness*, as she joined a pilgrimage to the Black Madonna of Czestochowa. 'There are thousands and thousands of people behind us waiting out in the rain, miles of pilgrims still arriving, kneeling, bowing, passing through the gates.' Nearly a million people converge each year from all over Poland, and walk for seven days to this ancient shrine, singing and praying.

When I see other people's feet at night in the first-aid stations, they are as bad as mine, and many are worse. Some women are walking these distances in high-heeled shoes, they have no others. Shoes are a very scarce commodity in Poland. There are people in wheelchairs ... One man in our group is eighty-two years old and has only a thin coat for protection – no tent, no food, only what he can find along the way or is given.

After the final mass at the shrine, she observes:

Now we are at the end, standing here in this chapel, laughing and crying, saying goodbye in a language I can't understand. How do you say goodbye to someone with whom you have stripped away all façades? The intensity of the walking has broken down all pretence, left us transparent ... if only more of us could walk with one another, singing and praying for days and days, if more of us could stop, there, towards the end, and say, 'I am sorry, please forgive me for anything I have done to hurt you; I am so sorry.'

Poland, indeed, has a remarkable history of pilgrimages which have continued for hundreds of years, unbroken by war or occupation. One occurs annually on 18 August, on the Feast of the Transfiguration of Jesus on the Mountain. From all over Poland people of the Eastern Orthodox faith literally bring their problems to God. Each pilgrim makes a large cross out of wood, on which he or she writes their requests, and then, shouldering it, sets off on foot to a mountain in the north east of Poland, which is believed to be holy.

More than 250 years ago thousands of people in this area died of cholera. Mass graves were dug and the plague seemed endless. Then, one night, an old man dreamed that he saw a Byzantine ikon of Mary telling him to gather people and go on foot to a particular mountain where they would be cured and the plague brought to an end. The next morning he told his parish priest about the dream. The priest assembled all those who could still walk and they set off journeying through forests and swamps, with many dying on the way. Finally they reached the mountain and those who arrived at the summit were indeed cured. From then onwards it was known as the Holy Mountain, and thousands more came from long distances to it to be cured, or to give thanks. The thousands of wooden crosses which today surround the church represent the prayers of many generations of pilgrims.

Each year the pilgrims arrive in their hundreds, singing hymns and popular songs. In the valleys round about, churches are ringing their bells. Each pilgrim arrives with a particular request – for a child, a member of the family or someone who is sick, for help with a problem, or for the unity of all Christians. Each pilgrim digs a hole and plants a cross in the ground. The services commence on the evening before, in the open air. Throughout the service the pilgrims enter the church, which is decorated with evergreens, to kiss the ikons of Mary, the Apostles and Saints, and kneel in prayer. Part of the service consists of a circular journey three times around the church, carrying a large ikon of Mary. People fall to the ground in prayer or follow it around on their knees in penitential manner. They then visit the graveyard to pray for the souls of the deceased. About midnight the priests return to the church and continue the liturgy through the night. Fires are lit outside from some of the old wooden crosses which have begun to rot, and many of the pilgrims sit up all night round the bonfires, huddled in blankets, while others gather in groups to keep vigil through the night, singing and praying. By the time the principal mass commences at eight o'clock in the morning, some 12,000 people have gathered.

However, in much of the Western world today, and even in such an ancient religious culture as Japan, many of the inherited beliefs are being discarded or fragmented. Carmen Blacker, in *The Catalpa Bow* records how in Japan there has been 'a loss of contact with the deity ... shrines degenerating into tourist attractions ... the 'other' world reduced to this world ... Though the vision remains it has lost its transforming power. No longer acknowledged to be a religious experience, it survives obscurely on the periphery of the religious world as a folk legend.' It is when a ritual loses its transforming power that it ceases to be a rite of passage. And yet, as has already been remarked, ancient forms are capable of being rediscovered, often in an unexpected way, as in the following account by one of my American students.

FROM ANJALI'S JOURNAL

There are a couple of things in the first chapter of *The Inner Stage* by James which really hit home and set me thinking and reflecting on an experience I had which was one of the real epiphanies of my life. It was very important to me. James comments, 'As a friend once remarked about Assisi, "Ultimately it is a place inside you. It is there, wherever you go."' A few pages later he talks about finding God both outside and inside of oneself, and how acting out an interior landscape sometimes is a way of finding the prayerful moment.

My epiphany was the product of a physical journey as well as a spiritual one. I would never have known that moment without the very physical aspect of the struggle which made it all a very *real experience*. I am Catholic, and went to the University of Dallas in Texas, a small, traditional, very rigorous and demanding school, affiliated with the Cistercians (who have a monastery in the grounds) as well as the Dominicans (who have a priory there). Part of the curriculum required that during the sophomore year the students study at our campus in Rome. During my year in Rome, the school took many trips around the country. One of the pilgrimages was to Assisi. It was a beautiful and peaceful town with a wonderful serenity about it. Though we saw so many of the historic holy places I was sadly not moved so much as I had hoped to be. I was going through a difficult time, a spiritual crisis, and was so beset with doubts and the presence of sin in my own life, that I could not respond as I wanted to. Then too, I loved St Francis (I was confirmed as Thomas Francis) and had hoped that being in Assisi would strike some sort of chord. It did not, and I was disappointed at the emptiness within me. I had felt much the same way at my confirmation a few years earlier, for I felt nothing happen, no change. They had told us that this was merely the outward symbol of the sacrament, that one day we would experience the sacrament in full and be confirmed inside by the Holy Spirit. We just had to be patient. Well, I am not a patient sort of person, and it sounded like a cop-out to me. Even the slap in the face by the priest which symbolized my willingness to suffer for God left me unaffected. So, now, in Assisi I felt the same way.

Our second day there, the priest who was in charge of the seminarians in our group announced that he would be saying mass not at the hotel but at another location, and that if we left by a certain gate and followed the road up into the hills, we would find him. He would begin the mass at 4 o'clock. Though we were welcome to attend mass at any of the churches in the town, he encouraged everyone to come to this one, even the non-Catholics in our group. Naturally we were all curious.

Early that afternoon I located the specified gate and set off down the narrow dirt road. I realized that the reason we were asked to walk was that our buses would never have been able to fit on that narrow road, nor would they have been able to negotiate the steep incline with all its curves. Indeed it was difficult even on foot. And it was hot. How far was this place, anyway? And what was it? I began to realize that as I didn't know what exactly my destination was, if I got lost I would not be able to ask for directions! Then, too, my Italian was not very good. No, it would be best not to get lost. But how did I know that I wasn't lost already? I kept walking. Occasionally I met up with a fellow student and for a while we would travel together, but as each had his own pace, we would inevitably split up.

I had been walking a very long time, perhaps an hour, when I saw a ramshackle building up ahead. It was a tavern, and seated at the long tables in front of it were several students who, tired and thirsty and discouraged by the unexpected hike, had turned aside to sit and drink in one another's company. They invited me to join them, and I would have given up and joined them had I had the money for a beer, but I didn't, and that alone allowed me to carry on. I soon left them behind. No doubt I would soon be there, wherever 'there' was. I had stripped off my winter coat by now, and my sweater was next. My T-shirt was soaked with sweat, and my breathing was getting more difficult. After another quarter of an hour I was almost certain I had made a mistake and that I should turn back. I passed my friend and room-mate, Nikki, who had been ill the previous year and had been paralysed. When she was recovering I used to support her going up and down the stairs at home. If *she* could do this, I thought, then so could I. I continued on, though by now every muscle in my body ached and I kept tripping over stones. My breathing grew more and more ragged, and the jarring in my gut at every step was more painful. Finally I knew I could go no further — why bother when I didn't even know where I was going or what lay ahead? Best to turn back, but that was equally impossible: I had no energy left to retrace my steps. I stood there, and in my frustration at the impasse, my anger at Father Fandle, my fear of being lost, and my utter fatigue, I could feel myself about to give way to tears.

At that moment, when I had reached my absolute limit, a little car appeared around the corner, slowly making its way up the hill along that treacherous road. It pulled up alongside me, stopped, and the door swung open. I did not even think (though I had never hitched a ride in my life) but climbed in. Inside was an Italian couple. They shut the door behind me and started driving again. 'Where are you going?' the woman asked in Italian. I shrugged, saying nothing. I only wished I knew, and how could I tell her the real problem when I lacked the words to express myself in her language? The man turned and looked at me and asked, 'Eremo?' The word was unfamiliar, meant nothing to me, but he was smiling. The woman smiled too and asked 'Eremo?'

'Eremo!' I found myself agreeing, returning their smile. 'Eremo!' We all repeated it several times, and though I did not know what this Eremo was, I very much wanted to go there. My mood had lifted, and I was refreshed and happy. They let me out at the next bend in the road and pointed at a path that led off between the trees. Before they drove off I shook their hands, saying 'A thousand, thousand many thank-yous, man and woman.' (It was the best I could manage in my limited vocabulary: '*Mille, mille molti grazie, signore e signora!*') Then they pointed at the path again, calling out 'Eremo!' one last time.

I set off down the path and soon came to a gate, passed through and found myself in a little compound of stone buildings on the edge of a cleft which fell away to a ravine far below. It was cool in this gash in the mountains, and the breeze felt wonderful on my soaking body. I heard cooing and glanced up to see a white dove perched on the very peak of the roof of the little chapel. I looked at my watch: it was nearly four o'clock. But I knew that I could not simply pass through that door. If I went in I would have to go all the way – I would not come out the same person. Behind and above me the doves were cooing, and I went in. The next hour ... I cannot tell you what precisely happened for, objectively, I guess, nothing did. But it was the most difficult and wonderful moment of my life. It was the day of my true and full confirmation at last.

I walked home with those others who had made it to the mass at the Hermitage or, rather ran, I should say. It was all downhill and could not have taken up more than forty-five minutes. Finally my heart was open to Assisi, which shall forever remain a sacred place for me. I attended mattins and vespers daily at the monastery for the remainder of our time there, and Assisi did indeed remain 'a place inside of me' for a long time.

However, I have lost it now and am having difficulty relocating it. I pray that I may find it again before I become so distracted that, like my friends at the tavern, I give up and cease to believe in a goal that lies so far ahead on an unknown road in a strange country. That experience in Assisi meant different things to different people, but to almost everyone who finished the difficult climb it meant something. Father knew what he was doing when he forced us to walk that difficult road to an unknown destination. The journey was as important for us to experience as the destination. James might call it a ritual journey, and indeed it was.

Anjali's account of her journey has all the characteristics of a pentitential pilgrimage. There are the difficulties of the journey, the narrow path, the steep and winding route; the physical exhaustion of the climb; the temptation to drop out, abandon the quest, and be seduced by the pleasure of the tavern on the wayside; her final despair when, utterly exhausted and lost, she is tempted to go back. It is then, at this moment of almost final surrender that, as in countless myths, help comes to her from outside, from strangers who, nonetheless, recognize her need and point her in the right direction. Finally she arrives at the *temenos*, the sacred space of St Francis's hermitage, in which the central rite and meaning of her journey is to take place. She pauses for a moment, having arrived at the exact hour at which mass is to be said. She has shed her defences (her outer garments) and is soaked to the skin; she is weary beyond belief, and yet knows that she has arrived at a predetermined time and place. She knows now, intuitively, that if once she crosses that threshold (*limen*) and enters that chapel, she will be transformed. When she emerges she knows that she will no longer be the same person. She makes her decision and enters the chapel. What happens during that hour is, she says, beyond words, but it is, at long last, her rite of passage, which should have happened at her confirmation but did not.

'Proclaim the pilgrimage among men. They will come to thee on foot and mounted on every kind of camel, lean on account of journeys through deep and distant mountains.' Throughout the history of world religions, mountains appear as places of holiness; from the sacred mountains of India, to those of Japan and that of Jerusalem. The meeting of Moses with God on the summit of Mount Sinai is an archetypal pattern which constantly repeats itself: 'I will ascend and go to Thy holy mountain . . . I have come to Thy holy mountain . . . Be true to the design which I showed thee on the mountain.'

IV

Circling the Mountain

More than a hundred of us, from Germany, France, Switzerland, Italy and the UK, as well as from all over the United States, had come to County Marin in California in response to an invitation from Anna Halprin to celebrate a ritual entitled *Circle the Mountain*. It was now the end of the week, the day after the ritual had been performed, and we were all seated under a tree, sheltering from the blazing sun, painting our response to the experience of the past week. One by one we held up our visualizations and said a few words about them. Suddenly it was Barbara's turn. In her sixties, with grey hair neatly plaited round her head, she was the wife of an Episcopalian minister. She began to explain her drawing. 'It has a broken heart,' she said, pointing to the figure she had drawn. All of a sudden her face crumpled and she was shaken with sobs. 'But it is alarmingly wide open.' Now she was laughing and crying simultaneously as she cried out, *'and the bird is definitely on its way!'* People like Barbara, and many more, are drawn into such ritual workshops because there is in them a hunger for more life, for something that they cannot find in their work, their church or their family. Especially is this so in America whose culture, as Harvey Cox has observed, is starved of rituals which can enable people to come to terms with the central crises in their lives.

I first met Anna Halprin in 1969, in San Francisco, and have long considered her one of the most important influences in theatre today, relating theatre to the needs of ordinary people, enabling them to create authentic life rituals. She is one of the few who is giving theatre back to people, enabling them to rediscover the origins of art. Sir Maurice Bowra, writing about primitive song and ritual, observed, 'Above all, it is an art and does what art always does for those who practise it with passion and devotion. It enables them to absorb experience with their whole natures and thereby fulfil a want which is fully satisfied neither by action nor by thought. In the end, like all true art, it enhances the desire and strengthens the capacity to live.'

More than thirty years ago Anna Halprin led one of the most dynamic and radical dance companies in America, the Dancers' Workshop, but she began to question the role of the audience in performance, as did Jerzy Grotowski in Poland and Peter Brook in England. In consequence she committed her life to working with non-professionals, seeking to unite personal growth with artistic growth, fusing life and art. She came to see that:

> Art grows directly out of our lives. Each person is his or her own art ... Whatever emotional, physical and mental barriers we carry around with us in our personal lives will be the same barriers that inhibit our full creative expression. It is for this reason that we need to release emotional blocks in order to realize fully our human creative potential in terms of being able to develop effectively as performers and as creators, as well as to participate with satisfaction in our lives. I look at emotional blocks as damaging to artistic growth. When a person has reached an impasse we know something in their life and in their art is not working.

The thrust of her work, and that of the Tamalpa Institute in Calfornia which she has formed, is towards unfolding every aspect of the individual within the creative community of a particular workshop, evolving rituals and ceremonials out of authentic life situations. 'I wish to extend every kind of perception,' wrote Anna in 1967, 'to involve people with their own environment so that life is lived as a whole.' To this end she sees the professional artist as no longer the solitary hero figure, 'but rather a special guide who works to evoke the art within us all.' In the late 1960s the Civil Rights movement in America escalated into a series of riots across the whole of the country. For Anna these riots were expressive of the stress and tension experienced by black people. She found herself wanting to use dance and theatre as social tools to bring about healthy changes. When she received an invitation from the director of a black arts centre in Watts to create a performance that would be given in the Los Angeles Mark Taper Theatre, she responded at once to this opportunity to explore the use of movement and creativity as a way of confronting and resolving the impasse of racial tension.

She conducted workshops, developing an all-black group in Watts, and an all-white group in San Francisco. After nine months the two groups were brought together to spend ten days and nights together in dance encounters before finally giving their public performance. 'We created our production,' she says, 'out of the real life encounters, conflicts, prejudices, inhibitions and different life styles of the two groups. We called the work, *Ceremony of Us!*' The process of creating the work was to prove as important as the performance itself. During one of the workshops in Watts, one of the men, Xavier Nash, wrote, 'My experience was like this orange that I just finished eating. I was whole, peeled, separated and consumed, and now I am whole again.' Similarly, during the performance, another member said, 'I see my life changing in *Ceremony of Us!* – thank God!' As Anna herself has remarked, '*Ceremony of Us!* changed all our lives.' In the same way, many who have worked in the theatre of Jerzy Grotowski, Eugenio Barba, Peter Brook and similar groups, would acknowledge that their lives have changed.

It is through the exercise of disciplines and skills, however simple, that people grow in an understanding of life and art. People are drawn into such workshops because there is in them a hunger for something that they cannot find elsewhere, especially in America. It is, as Carl Rogers observed, 'a hunger for relationships which are close and real; in which feelings and emotions can be spontaneously expressed without first being carefully censored or bottled up; where deep experiences – disappointments and joys – can be shared; where new ways of behaving can be risked and tried out; where an individual approaches the state where all is known and accepted; and thus further growth becomes possible'.

Over the past twenty years Anna Halprin and her colleagues have helped to create dance rituals for many occasions and situations. Sometimes they have been for a single person caught in a conflict within a relationship, or within themselves. Sometimes they have been for a group or a community. In her City Dance in 1977, more than 2000 people were involved throughout San Francisco, commencing at 4.30 am with a Fire Ceremony on the hilltops, and ending at dusk by the ocean. She has created rituals for young people moving from one school to another, involving their parents and teachers. She has created dances for 4000 elderly people at a conference on ageing – at which her ninety-four-year-old father suddenly got up out of his wheelchair and danced his own affirmation of his life.

In former times, as Anna says, communities knew how to celebrate and how to create rituals that would mark the movement from one stage of life to another. Today there are many more groups, especially in America, exploring ritual, but Anna Halprin has been a pioneer in this field. Today people come from all over the world to join in her search for living rituals and myths. The Tamalpa Institute has set in motion various projects, such as Positive Motion, which is an on-going group for men with AIDS, which uses the experiences of those involved to create rituals that meet their needs. One such work, *Carry Me Home*, was a thirty-minute dance ritual which evolved from material developed during the previous nine months. Its title was inspired by Brent Davis who, after a series of HIV-related illnesses, left the group to return to his small-town home in Texas. There is a similar group, Women with Wings, for women who are HIV positive. Another group Moving Towards Life, is part of a cancer self-help programme run by Anna Halprin and Jamie McHugh, which enables participants to confront and creatively cope with the challenges of living with cancer. As Jamie McHugh says, 'My personal experience demonstrated to me how vital the reclaiming of the body through movement is in the healing process. Illness can feel like such a profound betrayal by the body that we effectively begin to abandon ourselves and rely solely on outside interventions: doctors, medicines, treatments and so forth.'

The ritual I mentioned at the beginning of this chapter, *Circle the Mountain*, was spread over five years. From 1979 to 1981 a trail-side killer committed a series of brutal murders of young women on Mount Tamalpais, perhaps the most popular mountain in the United States and one that dominates the whole of County Marin in California. These murders terrified people in the Bay area and the mountain was closed for two years. At the time Anna and Laurence Halprin (her architect husband) were leading a workshop called A Search for Living Myths and Rituals. Anna began to notice that the image of the mountain kept recurring in people's visualizations and drawings, and she thought: What is this? It was apparent that there was a great deal of repressed rage, grief and impotence aroused by the murders. As a result it was decided to create a ritual with the aim of cleansing and reclaiming the mountain. On the day that it was carried out, helicopters circled the mountain, while police mingled with the crowds as the ritual progressed. A few days later the police received an anonymous call which led to the arrest of the killer, although the trial was to take five years and cost the taxpayers two million dollars. It was soon after this event that Don Jose Matsuwa, a 107-year-old Huichol and Indian shaman visited Anna and told her: 'The mountain is one of the most sacred places on earth, but for your ritual to be successful it must be repeated each year for five years. Only then will the mountain be purified.' And so each year the ritual was repeated with variations, moving from the theme of peace on the mountain to peace within the individual, the community, the world. Each year those taking part would make this dedication:

> For the spirit of the Mountain we dance,
> For those who consider her a holy place;
> For the Miwoks who lived beneath her,
> Gathered her herbs and sang her songs,
> We dance.
> And quietly we dance for those among us who have lost their
>   lives on her trails.
> Quietly we dance for them,
> For the trails that lead us back to the Mountain,
> We dance.

In 1985 the five-year cycle was completed, commencing on Easter Sunday with a series of runs to the summit of the mountain. Hundreds of people turned out for the various ceremonies, as Sufi,

Buddhist, Christian, Jewish and American Native Indian rituals were performed. Throughout the following week a hundred people worked each day and each night preparing the final ritual. People came from all over the world. All who wanted to take part were admitted even if they could not afford the modest fee. During the workshops they sought to find images that would express, and therefore exorcise, the killer within each one of them. I was invited by Anna to be present for the final rehearsal and performance.

The event took place in a huge gymnasium, with the spectators seated at one end on a series of bleachers. Those who had come to watch had not paid; they were not an audience in the usual sense, but were to be witnesses and participants in the ritual. They were not there to be entertained but to support and encourage by their presence. The hundred and more who were to perform lay about the floor of the gymnasium in recumbent forms. We, the witnesses, waited.

The ritual begins with dawn on the mountain. There is the cry of birds, the scurrying of small animals, and the soft sliding of snakes. Some of the performers sit still like rocks, or stand like trees. Then, at a signal, everyone is on the move. They begin circling the mountain, walking swiftly in and out of each other, forming a series of circles. They start to syncopate the movement. Linking arms they swirl, change direction, hold up their arms, clap their hands, shout, cry out, but always on the move, straining now to gain the summit. They form different groups, dissolving and reforming, with endless variations of rhythm and pattern. Tunnels are formed: some are dragged through, others slide. Some are carried on the shoulders of partners. Here one person improvises and others form a group around her; there a lone figure dances on his own. As the music reaches a climax they all form a central cluster like a swarm of bees, while one individual from within the group is thrust up high, poised on one leg, the other leg and both arms extended, like a bird in flight: 'The bird is definitely on its way.'

The next section marks the unleashing of the monster, the killer within each of us. The performers line up in ranks at the far end. They extend their arms sideways and, raising their thighs and stomping their feet, advance slowly towards the witnesses. Then, at a signal, the first line charges, roaring and screaming, faces distorted with hate. Simultaneously, we the witnesses lift white masks to our faces and become faceless monsters. The first charge collapses in front of the first row of witnesses. There follows the second charge, then a third, a fourth, and a fifth, until finally the hundred or more bodies are piled up, groaning, sweating, emotionally drained. The music is solemn and slow as they arise, gazing into each other's eyes, acknowledging their hatred and anger, that they have been capable of it. Many hold each other in an embrace of two or three or even more. Quite spontaneously and remarkably, we, too, the witnesses, turn to each other in a gentle embrace. This is no simulated emotion but emotion summoned deep from within each person there.

Now the performers create an arch under which we all pass, witnesses too. We emerge into a large circle formed by the dancers, and then on through another human arch, and enter what appears like a vast cathedral. This is an image only, but everyone seems to share this sense of having passed through a narrow defile and entered an awesome but joyous space. Many as they enter it twirl and turn with a sense of release, recalling the Shaker hymn:

> And when we find ourselves in the place just right
> 'Twill be in the valley of love and delight.
> To turn, turn, will be our delight,
> Till by turning, turning, we come round right.

A father walks through with his two small daughters, holding each by the hand; a mother sets down her child to run free; tough guys, shy solitaries, grandparents, whole families, gay couples, a Buddhist priest – it is as though all humanity were entering some vast cathedral of the imagination. It is the calm after the storm, recalling that most beautiful of all Martha Graham's dance rituals, *Ardent Song* only here created by and made accessible to ordinary people.

At breakfast the next morning, seated on the terrace of Anna's house, high above the treetops, overlooking the Bay, Anna speaks of the need to bring these people gently down to earth. 'Now they all want to go on performing the piece, but it isn't a theatre work, and, besides, they could not sustain that kind of emotion. It is a ritual created for a specific time, place, purpose, and shared with a specific group of people.' We discuss how there are three stages to the creation of a ritual: the preparation, the performance and the dispersal. The latter is perhaps the most important and I suggest to her that it is the age-old question of learning how to come down from the mountain of vision and re-enter the plains of reality in order to continue one's own journey, enriched by the experience of communion with one another, and yet not hanging on to a womb-like dependence of clinging to the group or to the experience. Anna thinks that she will lead them first in individual visualizations, drawing and painting, and then take them to the ocean and get them to build structures on the shore, to help objectify where each is going, and in this way help to internalize the whole process for them, integrating it into the lives. A ritual is like a door in a wall which leads us into a secret garden. Within that garden we walk in another space and time. It is an enchanted garden. But we have also to emerge from that garden, and so there has to be a gate to let us out so that we can return to the ordinary world. Just as in a Buddhist hall of meditation, for the zasen there is a special ceremony for entering and taking one's place for meditation, so also there is a special ceremony for concluding the meditation.

'I believe in art as an enduring process,' observed Anna that morning. 'For it touches on the spiritual dimension in a way that no other human activity does. In art you are able to give expression to that which lies deep inside you.' Ritual is one of the neglected forms of theatre. Although certain rituals are timeless, perfected and handed down across the centuries in the form of the great liturgies of the major faiths, and are capable always of rediscovery, other rituals need to be created for a specific time, place and need. A true testing of a ritual is when a strong presence of performers and a strong presence of witnesses 'can produce a circle of unique intensity in which barriers can be broken and the invisible becomes real', and it is when these two worlds meet that 'there is a burning and fleeting taste of another world, in which our present world is integrated and transformed'. Those are the words of the British theatre director, Peter Brook, and recall something that Martha Graham once said to me: 'In my work I have always sought to reveal an image of man in his struggle for wholeness, for what one might call God's idea of him rather than man's idea of himself.'

Peter Brook once asked an Indian actor his secret, and he replied: 'I try to bring together all that I have experienced in my life, so as to make what I am doing a witness for what I have felt and what I have understood.' It is when a community of individuals bring to the creation and enactment of a ritual such a total dedication that then the invisible becomes real:

> For you I have come out of myself
> To perform life without a mask ...
> At the deepest level of myself.

V

Emily's Journey

The majority of people possess, no matter how unused, real creative and imaginative faculties, and today the individual needs to discover how to give form to his or her most urgent feelings and aspirations, so that she or he may the better understand themselves or others. We have to learn how to respond directly and truly to our deepest impulses and to give them form and rhythm, above all in our forms of worship, like the youth Tito who, at the close of Herman Hesse's *The Glass Bead Game*, quite unselfconsciously, begins to dance on the mountain-top as the sun rises: 'Without knowing what he was doing, asking no questions, he obeyed the command of the ecstatic moment, danced his worship, prayed to the sun, professed with devout movements and gestures his joy, his faith in life.' Such a ritual is spontaneous, private, of the immediate moment. Other rituals arise out of the ancient traditions of an individual's culture as in this example from Kathleen Raine's final volume of autobiography, *India Seen Afar*: 'I have on more than one occasion watched Santosh dance her Geeta Radha-Krishna dances. It heals something in Santosh when she dances Radha. She goes every morning to Triveni before she starts her day's work, and says she could not live her life or do her work without these hours on the dance floor with her guru, who teaches her more than dance, teaches the deep realities of the soul's life.'

While the major religions continue to offer their ancient rituals and pilgrimages to the faithful, there are countless thousands of people who have no tradition and who yet have a need to create rituals and to go on pilgrimage in an ever-recurring quest for meaning. One such ritual and pilgrimage was created one summer in Michigan for Emily Stuart, a dancer, who had to leave halfway through a six-week summer course which I was leading at Grand Rapids.

The basic structure was agreed upon by the group but without Emily being present or informed. She chose to go off on her own and to create her own contribution. The ritual was to express the group's farewell to Emily as well as her farewell to it. Once the basic structure, which was to take the form of a journey, had been agreed, the detail was left to each individual and not known in advance. It was agreed that it should take place out of doors and that I would act as Emily's guide throughout the ritual.

On the day itself Emily was blindfolded and led to an area of woodland where the others were waiting. She arrived, carrying in her arms an enormously heavy sack which, she said, was the burden that she chose to carry on her journey, and that inside the sack were her gifts for the rest of us. We came to a path that led through the woods and here, removing Emily's blindfold, I invited her to sit down, resting her burden, while I bathed her feet, and spoke for her the poem, *Ithaca*, by C.P. Cafavy:

When you set out on your journey to Ithaca,
Then pray that the road is long, full of adventure, full of
    knowledge . . .
Always keep Ithaca fixed in your mind.
To arrive there is your ultimate goal.
But do not hurry the voyage at all.
It is better to let it last long years;
And even to anchor at the isle when you are old,
Rich with all that you have gained on the way,
Not expecting that Ithaca will offer you riches.
Ithaca has given you the beautiful voyage.
Without her you would never have taken the road.
But she has nothing more to give you.
And if you find her poor, Ithaca has not defrauded you.
With the great wisdom you have gained, with so much
    experience,
You must surely have understood by then what Ithaca means.

The journey was then resumed. At a bend in the path one of the group stepped forward with a large basket which he handed to Emily so that she could place her burdens in it. At different stages along the journey others appeared, offering gifts of fruit and flowers, bread and wine. Together the group arrived at an open meadow where Emily was relieved of her burdens and invited to lie down on a parachute in which she was then carried. Finally she stepped out from it, and it was elevated above her like a canopy, until the group arrived at a tree at the foot of which a fire was burning. Here a ritual washing of hands took place, and then everyone climbed up into the tree to share a simple meal. Quite spontaneously someone began to sing some words from a Robert Frost poem, which developed into a round:

> And I have miles to go before I sleep,
> And miles to go before I sleep.

Now Emily said that she would like to give us her gifts but first we must climb down. The parachute was spread out neatly and we were invited to form a circle with our eyes closed while she prepared her image of what the past weeks had meant for her. We began to sing the AH sound, one of the vocal exercises that we used daily, the energy coursing through the group, the sound rising and falling, like an onward-flowing stream. When I opened my eyes I saw in the centre of the parachute, which was ringed round by the standing figures of all of us, a circle of fine pale sand collected from the river bed and, placed neatly on it, a smaller circle of twelve beautifully shaped stones, in the centre of which was one large pear-shaped stone. The image was totally unexpected and moving. The breeze stirred the leaves of the tree under which we were standing and sent its shadows flickering across us as the singing grew in intensity, expressing our response to Emily's mandala. In turn each person stooped to pick up a stone, the one towards which each felt drawn. As the singing swelled I had the feeling that the stone in the centre was meant for me and yet I held back lest this be egotistical on my part. Finally, however, when all the stones had been taken and only the one in the centre remained, I recognized that everyone else sensed this was intended for me. As I lifted it, I brushed off the loose sand and, kneeling in front of

Emily, placed the stone in her hand, offering it to her. Gently she caressed my head. Yet even as I lifted the stone from its bed of sand I had been aware that there was something underneath it, half buried, like a small white serpent. As the group continued singing, Emily stooped and dug it out.

It was a small stone with a hole bored through the centre threaded through which was a loop of cord. Lifting it up, Emily moved towards me. Aware of what was about to happen, I bowed my head as she placed this stone locket round my neck. The singing surrounded us like a waterfall, powerful and strong, as I reached up and held her in my arms. She relaxed, sighing deeply. Then I released my arms and hands, letting her go. Slowly she moved round the circle, embracing each person in turn and, at the end, walked out of the circle – which immediately closed up – so that she was now standing outside, at a distance from the whole experience of the past three weeks. She had said her farewell and made her exit. We also had said farewell to Emily, knowing that we must continue working without her. The ritual was at an end. Suddenly there were loud cheers. There was a sudden release of gaiety as we formed a cheerful, festive procession, newspaper banners unfurling in the breeze, flute and recorder playing, as we wound our way back to the studio.

Long afterwards Emily Stuart wrote to me from Indiana about the experience of this Ritual of Farewell. 'My arms ached for days with the weight of those stones, but I would not have had it otherwise. They were a burden I chose to carry and what I wanted to give, for I had received so much. I am content.'

To speak of an outer journey and an inner journey is perhaps to suggest two separate journeys, as though one were trying to travel parallel paths, or changing from path to path. In reality there is only one journey, for every journey we take is, potentially, also an inner voyage of discovery. Had Emily Stuart not journeyed from Indiana to take part in a summer course on theatre and ritual, she would not have found that very potent mandala which she now carries with her always. The creative process, says Jung, consists in the unconscious activation of an archetypal image, and in elaborating and shaping that image into a finished work. So, within a ritual created for her by the group, Emily found her way, through a ritual of her own devising, to the archetype of the stone, which we find in the Revelation of St John. 'To those who have won the victory I will give some·of the hidden meaning. I will also give each of them a white stone, on which a real name is written, which no one knows except the one who receives it.' The purpose of a myth is to enable us to hold in balance our conscious and unconscious lives, the inner and the outer. Once we learn to accept the symbols that well up within us we are made aware of an invitation to live life at a deeper level than it is lived every day.

VI

Sacred Ritual

Religious ideas are always and everywhere symbolic truths. They can never be understood in a rational way alone. Every religious symbol when it originated was an *experience* surpassing conscious knowledge. It is only when religion becomes established that symbols are then worked into dogmas by the conscious intellect. An objective rational interpretation of art or of a religious experience is of little value unless there is also a subjective and intuitive identification with the material under examination. Thus the paintings, those extraordinary mandalas, of Dame Hildegarde of Bingen, the twelfth-century mystic, erupted first from her unconscious; only afterwards did she meditate upon them, and write down her meditations. The danger is that our society has largely lost touch with the art of thinking in images. 'Our thinking is largely discursive, verbal, linear', as Joseph Campbell observed in his television series, *The Power of Myth*, 'yet there is more reality in an image than in a word.' Similarly Jung remarked in reference to symbols, 'Their pregnant language cries out to us that they mean more than they say.'

At its most intense, ritual leads us into worlds not realized and becomes sacred. There is a remarkable example of this in Oliver Sacks's book *The Man Who Mistook His Wife For a Hat*, in which he describes Jimmy G., one of the patients at the neurological hospital in New York where Sacks worked. Admitted in 1975 at the age of 49 it was found that Jimmy could remember everything up to 1945 but everything after that date had been wiped from his memory. Such memory loss is known as Korsakov's Syndrome.

47

Sacks wrote to Professor A.R. Luria, one of the leading Russian neurologists, asking his opinion. Luria replied:

There are no prescriptions in a case like this. Do whatever your ingenuity and your heart suggest. There is little hope or no recovery in his memory. But a man does not consist of memory alone. He has feeling, will, sensibilities, moral being, matters of which neuropsychology cannot speak. And it is here, beyond the realm of an impersonal psychology, that you may find ways to touch him, and change him. And the circumstances of your work allow this, for you work in a Home, which is like a little world, quite different from the clinics and institutions where I work. Neuropsychologically there is little or nothing that you can do; but in the realm of the Individual there may be much that you can do.'

Sacks, finding that he tends to speak of Jimmy as 'a lost soul' wonders whether, in fact, Jimmy has been 'desouled' by the disease. 'Do you think he *has* a soul?' he asks one of the sisters. 'Watch Jimmy in chapel and judge for yourself,' is the reply. He does so and is deeply moved to observe in Jimmy an intensity and a steadiness of attention and concentration that he has never witnessed before or even conceived him capable of having. He watches him kneel and take the sacrament upon his tongue.

Fully, intensely, quietly, in the quietude of absolute concentration and attention, he entered and partook of the Holy Communion. He was wholly held, absorbed, by a feeling. There was no forgetting, nor Korsakov's then, nor did it seem possible or imaginable that there should be; for he was no longer at the mercy of a faulty and fallible mechanism but was absorbed in an act of his whole being which carried feeling and meaning in an organic continuity and unity, a continuity and unity so seamless it could not permit any break. Clearly Jimmy had found himself . . . in the absoluteness of spiritual attention and act. The Sisters were right – he did find his soul there. And so was Luria whose words came back to me, 'A man does not consist of memory alone. He has feeling, will, sensibilities, a moral being . . . It is here you may touch him and see a profound change.'

It was in an act of worship, at the centre of a sacred ritual, that Jimmy 'found himself'.

Central to our understanding of sacred ritual is the meaning of worship. The word itself comes from the word *weorp*, meaning worth or value, esteem, honour, dignity, and so veneration of a power considered divine, the adoration of a superior being. Worship is the expression of belief, but even more of faith, in a superior being. All sacred ritual, indeed all ritual, should give expression to the deepest yearning within us, urging us towards something which always remains beyond us. But worship is more than a feeling. To worship is to do, and a ritual is an act, but for worship to be truly meaningful it must permeate our whole lives and make them meaningful.

'In too many churches public worship has become almost entirely cerebral and verbal,' writes Bill Jardine Grisbrooke, 'and that in an age which is particularly attracted to, and conditioned by, the visual, cannot but be counter-productive, in terms of both spirituality and popularity.'

Similarly in a symposium, *English Catholic Worship*, Christopher Walsh writes of a crisis of credibility which he links with a crisis of symbolism, and observes, 'Unlike words, symbols speak to our whole personality, not just to our ears and intelligences, they create resonances and associations inaccessible to words, they appeal to intuition and experience as much as to understanding. And their power is incomparably greater than any words.'

Recently I attended an Anglican Easter liturgy which observed all the external rubrics − that is, the written text and form − but which failed entirely to embody, or give expression to the inner meaning of the text. I came away deeply *dis*-spirited instead of *in*-spirited. Although the form had been piously observed the spirit itself was absent; 'the god' was not at home. If only, I thought, the organ had burst forth with triumphal chords, or fireworks had exploded, and bells pealed, all proclaiming: '*Christ is Risen!*' I could not help thinking of Eleanor Munro's description of the Orthodox Church's Holy Fire Ceremony in the Church of the Holy Sepulchre in Jerusalem, one of the oldest equinoctial ceremonies in the world, going back at least 4000 years to the Indo-Iranian fire worship rituals.

The Holy Fire Ceremony, which culminates at noon on the Saturday before the Orthodox Easter, opens with a stunning procession of bejewelled and robed ecclesiastics. One of them is then stripped of his finery and goes alone into the empty tomb. Its door is sealed off and all the lights in the building, vaults, domes and galleries are doused. For an hour or so a band of excited youths whirl, leap and shout around the Tomb: Christ's dancing dervishes churning life back into it. When they finally bound away, silence falls. Not a soul stirs among the hundreds of pilgrims packed in and waiting. And then suddenly – fire is seen to pass out of the two portholes in the Tomb onto torches held by two deacons who in turn rush it off to local churches . . . At the same moment, in the church itself, fire seemed to *leap* – or to have leapt – from candle to candle in people's hands until it fills the whole church with its miracle light . . . With a sudden rush the whole basin of the church, every corner to the farthest reach of it, seems to have caught fire at once, thousands of candles flaring up in thousands of hands as if at one stroke; it's impossible not to be shaken. Then people are crying, *Kyrie Eleison*, and *Christos Anesti*! Bells are ringing, chimes and gongs are sounding. 'I have come to bring fire,' Christ said. By noon on Saturday in Jerusalem even a sceptic may feel that some such release of energy has taken place.

It may be argued that it is easier to create such a liturgy or sacred ritual in a huge church packed with a vast crowd, but it is not so. I think back often to an Easter liturgy created by John Hencher, an Anglican priest, one Easter Saturday evening in a redundant twelfth-century church in Herefordshire. There was no electricity and we had been warned to bring torches so that we could find our way through the darkened churchyard. Inside the building the pews had been arranged around the walls so that there was a large central space. Some sixteen people, not all of whom were believers, had been invited. On our arrival we found a single candle burning in the church.

Each of us quietly found a place to sit and then waited. The one candle was extinguished. Seated in the darkness of that ancient church we were led in a meditation upon the physical darkness in the building, then to the darkness in South Africa, in Europe and elsewhere and, finally, in our own hearts. We sat in silence, meditating. Suddenly, from behind the stone altar a sheet of flame leaped up, like a wall of fire, and the words 'Christ is Risen!' were proclaimed. Now John Hencher moved towards us, bearing in one hand a lighted candle and in the other hand a basket of candles for us to take one and light it from his. As each one of us sat, holding a lighted candle and gazing at its fragile flame, we were led into a meditation upon light, shining now in the darkness, upon the light in the world wherever goodness is to be found, and lastly upon the light in our own hearts. Again we rested in silence. Then we were invited to stand in a circle, holding our candles, repeating the words 'Christ is Risen!' We listened to some words written by Alice Meynell:

> Public was the Death;
> But Power and Might,
> But Life again, and Victory,
> Were hushed within the dead of night.
> The shutter'd dark, the secrecy,
> And all alone, alone, alone –
> He rose again behind the stone.

Music – some Bach? – began to play as we gave each other a kiss of peace. Then, arm in arm, in twos and threes, we began to move about the space, taking our lighted candles into the furthermost corners of the building. We were all strangers to one another and yet united by this simple celebration of Easter. As we left, the farmer's wife, who lived in the farm alongside the church, shouted out to us across the darkness, 'Wasn't that a lovely service? I've never been to such a service before!' On that Easter Eve, in that ancient church, we had been led out of the darkness of pain and suffering into the joy of the light, experiencing within ourselves the dying and resurrection which is at the heart of Easter. In that group there was one atheist, a few agnostics and a core of Christians, but all had clearly shared in a depth of communion which is all too rare nowadays in our churches and synagogues. We returned to the home of John Hencher to be given a meal and to share further in the breaking of bread.

As Victor Turner wrote, rituals may become mere husks at certain historical junctures but this state of affairs belongs to the senescence or pathology of the ritual process, not to its normal working. What the churches, and indeed all the major faiths, need to realize is the necessity to evolve new rituals as well as to rediscover the ancient rites. John X. Herriott, in one of the last pieces he wrote for *The Tablet* spoke of the need for 'rites that reflect and express realities as they are experienced now, and the insight of our own times, not a regression to past ages'. On reading this I was reminded of an unusual request I once received from an elderly woman, a pensioner in the North of England, whom I had never met but who used to write to me. She was, she wrote on this occasion, deeply troubled by the sins of her past life and weighed down by the burden of guilt. Might she make her confession to me in writing? Now correctly speaking such a person should be directed to their own parish priest. However, as I knew from her letters, not only was she not on a bus route, but no one from the local church ever went near her. She was elderly, fragile of health. I also had to consider the fact that she had chosen to write to me as a priest, feeling in some intuitive way that she needed me to intervene or mediate on her behalf. So I wrote back, suggesting that she write out her confession and place it in a sealed envelope. I would not read it but, on the following Sunday, at the early-morning Eucharist, I would burn it at the time of the General Confession and, as I gave Absolution to all those present in the church so, also, I would give it to her.

The following Sunday I took with me to the church a wok which I placed at the centre of the altar. I explained to the congregation what I was going to do and used the story in my homily to illustrate the need in all of us to let go of the past: to forgive is to give way, give away, let go. Only in this way can we grow and change, set free from the burden of the past. Then the congregation began the General Confession:

Almighty God ... we acknowledge and bewail our manifold sins and wickedness which we from time to time most grievously have committed, by thought, word and deed, against Thy Divine Majesty, provoking most justly Thy wrath and indignation

against us. We do earnestly repent, and are heartily sorry
for these our misdoings; the remembrance of them is grievous
unto us; the burden of them is intolerable. Have mercy upon us
... forgive us all that is past, and grant that we may evermore
serve and please Thee in newness of life...

As they did so, I held up the sealed envelope to the flame of one of
the candles on the altar. As it caught fire I placed it in the wok to
burn. Then, as I gave the Absolution, 'Almighty God ... have
mercy upon you, pardon and deliver you from all your sins;
confirm and strengthen you in all goodness; and bring you to
everlasting life, through Jesus Christ, our Lord ...' so I reached
out to this woman, knowing that she was indeed 'present' at that
moment. As she wrote afterwards, it was for her 'a deeply healing
experience', as it was for all those present on that morning.

True ritual should indeed *set fire* to us all. Fire is an image of
great potency and yet all too easily in churches it has become a
cosy, sentimental image, just as so much Christian worship has
become genteel, safe and bourgeois. Not idly did Jesus say, 'I have
come to bring fire and what will I but that it be multiplied.' The
image used of the descent of the Holy Spirit at Pentecost is of
individual tongues of fire descending upon each person who, when
touched by it, suddenly understand one another, speaking the
language of the heart.

We long to speak heart to heart, to be set fire to, to come alive,
to live authentically. Sometimes at the start of a workshop I ask
people why they have come. 'I feel I am not creative, not expressing myself,' replies one; while another may say, 'I want to learn
how to be expressive through my body, to be less cerebral'; or 'I
want to get in touch with my real self, to use my body like an
instrument.'

If sacred ritual is to come alive it must be through the imagination
and through meditation. The Christian churches celebrate a season
called Advent, which is the period leading up to Christmas, but
although there are readings and prayers for this season, Sunday by
Sunday, few Christians really reflect deeply upon them, or integrate into their lives what is happening. I was made aware of this
in an unexpected way one year in my former home in Wales,

where I had a chapel in the cellar. It had been my usual practice on Christmas Eve to take a life-size image of a baby, moulded in clay, and lay it in a basket before the altar, placing a white linen cloth on top. Then, on Christmas morning, the 'baby' would be laid on the altar itself, a great slab of thick Welsh slate. On this particular Christmas Eve I found myself gazing at the shape of the baby under the cloth; this led me to meditate upon Mary's pregnancy. It was then that I realized how little thought we give during Advent to those nine months when Jesus was being carried in his mother's womb. As a result, at the beginning of each Advent thereafter, I would place the baby in the basket, with the cloth over it, and take this image as the focal point for my meditation. The danger with so many devotions is that we lose sight of the simple earthy images, of a woman carrying the weight of her child on the long journey up into the hills to visit her cousin, Elizabeth, who is also pregnant; feeling the child inside her and yet not fully understanding what is happening to her. Whether we accept the story of Jesus's virgin birth as fact or as a symbol, we shall be led to meditate upon the great archetype of the Mother, she who is also the figure of Sophia, Wisdom, who, we read, was with God at the beginning of time, before the world began. The great archetype of the Mother also teaches us to address God as Mother, as She as well as He. We need images, symbols, pictures, as a way of approaching 'the ground of our being', while accepting that in the spiritual growth of a human being, whatever our religious tradition, all images come eventually to be discarded. Images that once served our need are shed; as Robert Frost once wrote, 'We grow by shedding.' New images may take the place of old until perhaps we reach that place where images are no longer needed, when we come to that inner cave of stillness and silence.

SACRED SPACES

In any discussion of ritual, and especially of sacred ritual, one has to consider the element of space. Certain spaces are more suitable than others. The same is true of a party: if there is too much space, and no focus or structure for the party, then its energy is liable to be dissipated. One of the major factors contributing to a lack of the sense of the numinous in so many modern churches is that few architects have considered the principles of sacred geometry. The traditional structure of cathedrals provided a large central space, without chairs, suitable for public worship, but with a series of chapels on each side where individual worshippers could go apart and pray, or a small congregation gather for an early mass. Such spaces also provided, intuitively, for the individual needs of the worshipper, the smaller spaces of the side chapels appealing to the more introverted, and the larger central area to the more extroverted. People respond differently to space. Barbara Hepworth, the British sculptor, once told me how she loved to sit in St Mark's Square in Venice, and watch the way in which tourists, entering that huge piazza, would respond: some would keep to the perimeter and work their way round, while others would stride boldly into the centre, like a matador entering the ring.

Finally, in traditional churches and cathedrals there would be, beyond the nave, and often behind a screen, the chancel with its high altar approached by a series of steps, recalling the words of the psalmist: 'I will go up even unto the altar of God.' As the congregation moved forward for the reception of the eucharist so there would have been a sensation of ascent, of going up to the holy of holies.

Such an inner sanctum is to be found in synagogues, in the Orthodox Church and in Hindu temples. We do not worship solely with our minds but with our whole beings. In worship we need a sense of space, of height and depth and breadth, of intimacy and of distance, mirroring the spaces within us. I think of those words of Jeremy Taylor: 'There should be in the soul halls of space, avenues of leisure, and high porticos of silence where God walks.'

In all religions one finds a *temenos*, a sacred or purified space, separated from the profane world outside, into which the deity may be safely inducted. A place of worship should be like a mandala, that powerful symbol for isolating and enclosing space which is also a symbol of the womb in which the disciple or initiate is newly conceived and grows. Stepping across the threshold of a holy place we enter into another region where time and eternity, God and humans meet. I recall attending a Buddhist meditation in a private house in the woods in northern Michigan. From the moment of arrival we were conscious of crossing a threshold as we were quietly greeted by our hostess and invited to remove our shoes ('The ground whereon thou walk'st is holy ground'), before entering the room set aside for meditation. This inner room was lit only by candlelight; at one end was a statue of the Buddha to which, as in all halls of meditation, we bowed; bowing not in worship but acknowledging the Buddha within each of us. A gong announced and also closed the period of meditation. As we departed we bowed to our place of meditation, to the Buddha and to the room. Such a simple ritual of obeisances, of shedding one's footgear, of speaking quietly, of silence, emphasizes that one is crossing over into a sacred space.

Even Quakers who appear to reject all external rituals have, in fact, a very ritualized form for their meeting for worship. Chairs are set in a circle around a table, usually circular, on which stands a bowl of flowers, even a candle. The circular bowl, the circular table, the circle of chairs, within the square of the room, are in themselves a mandala. Meetings for worship commence at 11 am but ten or fifteen minutes beforehand, individual Friends will enter and quietly sit with closed eyes. Slowly the room fills up with people in an ever-deepening silence. Then, on the stroke of eleven, the meeting formally commences, and the silence continues until someone is 'moved' to speak. A whole hour of vibrant silence can go by without anyone speaking. If someone does rise to speak (their eyes closed), the rest listen (also with closed eyes) until that person has finished. No one rises to answer. There is silence. No one else may be moved to speak or it may be another quarter of an hour before someone rises to speak. On the stroke of twelve the meeting for worship is ended and everyone moves out for the social ritual of coffee and chat.

A prototype of all holy places is the Temple of Tiruvannamalai, one of the most beautiful temples in southern India, which covers about twenty-five acres and consists of a central sanctuary surrounded by three courtyards, each enclosed by a high wall, each housing many shrines. The innermost enclosure of all holds the sanctuary of Shiva himself. Henri le Saux, a French Benedictine monk who founded the first Christian ashram in India and took the name of Abhishiktananda, spent many months at a time alone in one of the caves of the sacred Mountain of Arunachala, and was eventually permitted to enter this holy of holies: 'The silence and the darkness made this sacred and numinous place even more impressive. Finally, our circle [of the outer shrines] completed, and the world of images having been left behind, we entered the sanctuary itself ... a dark square chamber where, bare and solitary, stands the upright stone of the Shiva lingam, dimly lit by an oil lamp, the sign of the presence of the Lord Arunachala in the midst of his people, and the pledge of his grace.'

It was in one of the many caves in Mount Arunachala that Abhishiktananda spent long periods in meditation. There was only a recess for sitting cross-legged, it was impossible to stand upright. At the back of the cave was an opening along which he could wriggle like a snake and which led to a chamber 6 feet high and 6 feet wide. 'This hidden cave,' he wrote in *The Secret of Arunachala*, 'conveyed an amazing sense of mystery. It recalled all the old myths of the Earth Mother, the fruitful source of life. One could only enter this shrine alone and stripped of all clothing, like a child in its mother's womb, and there the whole mystery of divine rebirth was evoked and that through signs which were so powerful that they seemed almost sacramental.' It was in this innermost cave that Abhishiktananda wrote in his journal for 25 December, 1953: 'Christmas in the depth of the heart, at the heart of Arunachala, sang first Vespers and Mattins of Christmas!'

But how difficult it is in the West to find such holy places or spaces. They do exist and can be found, but with difficulty.

INDIVIDUAL MILESTONES

All experiments in sacred ritual should be pragmatic, created for individual needs, times and circumstances. Once, faced with a couple who had been living together for some years but who had come to me asking me to marry them in church, I found myself asking each of them to write me a letter, separately and without consulting each other, saying why they felt this need. After all, I asked, why did they not simply get married in a registry office? Sally wrote to me as follows: 'Rituals I have come to believe are very important in our lives. They mark the milestones we pass, and should be acknowledged. I believe it is time to acknowledge and celebrate my relationship with Charlie.' She went on to describe her own background: parents married in church, three children of whom she was the youngest, and then, when she was six, her parents divorced. Her mother married again, had another child, and then separated from her second husband. Now they are together again. Sally's father remarried, had two more children, then divorced, and married a third time. 'I hope this short history of my family,' wrote Sally, 'is an adequate explanation of why I never thought of marriage as being very important, particularly when it came to children. However, after living with Charlie for several years and believing that we will continue to share our lives, I have come to a new understanding of what marriage can mean.'

In this letter Charlie wrote, 'I think that in a ritual it is possible, both through the spoken vows of mutual commitment and through the gathering together of many of the people amongst whom we both live and work, to affirm and celebrate that which has joined our lives so closely together. I also feel the need to both honour and celebrate and recognize the spiritual, unseen elements of our relationship. Above all, perhaps, I need also to acknowledge an authority beyond myself and beyond the immediate and often care-worn world. I look to find a connection to that which binds people together for the best purposes: for mutual support, care and growth; a widening of perception and a recognition of the importance of this in relation to the infinite world around us.'

The ritualizing of an experience is essentially a creative act in which one takes the broken pieces of one's life and assembles them into a mosaic of meaning, creating, as Robert Frost once expressed it, 'one more stay against confusion'. But it only becomes a healing or integrating influence when we continue to meditate upon it, to live with it, and to absorb it into our daily living. We need to experience such images in the depths of our being, for both wisdom and grace reach us by many different routes, but most of all in the silence of our own meditation.

As I have said, so many visiting our churches and other places of worship are alienated by what they find, wondering what relevance it has to their own lives. To what extent do these rituals reflect an interior reality? Too many clergy, in America and Britain, of all denominations, seem wholly unaware of what it is they are enacting. Although Christians of the Roman and Episcopalian and Anglican traditions are taught that the mass or eucharist is valid however it is celebrated, we do need to ponder the way in which these liturgies are celebrated. It is significant that when a man or woman of holiness officiates, the ritual is always transformed, and the word becomes a living word. I am reminded, as so often, of the words of P. D. Mehta, in *The Heart of Religion*:

In the hands of the great ceremonialists these rituals produced psychological effects. *Trained to meditate*, the attention of the skilled celebrant was wholly concentrated upon the psychospiritual significance of the ritual. It was the power of concentrated thought of the celebrant and of the devout feelings of the participants which made the atmosphere of the ceremony, exerted the influence for uplift and inner vision in the congregation, and made the ritual a veritable sacrament, a ceremonial magic. The actual presence and benediction of the invoked and worshipped deity was deeply felt. Such magic was essentially a communion with the divine and with nature. The esteem in which the efficacy of the sacrificial ritual was held was expressed in superlative terms by some of the greatest Upanishadic teachers.

Is it surprising, therefore, that so often those who are in search of truth and love and meaning and the divine, turn away in frustration from our churches? As Sir Laurens van der Post has confessed:

Fewer and fewer of us can find [religious awareness] any more in churches and temples and the religious establishments of our time. Much as we long for the churches to renew themselves and once more become, in contemporary idiom, an instrument of the pentecostal spirit, many of us now have to testify that, despite the examples of dedicated men devoted to their theological vocations, they have failed to give modern man a living experience of religion such as I and others have found in the desert and the bush of Africa.

VII

Death and Ritual

Before we can create new rituals for the dying and the dead we have first to come to terms with our own dying and death. Faced with another person's death we are always reminded of our own chronicles of wasted time. Like Longfellow we realize that for all our achievements and honours, small or great, we 'leave behind us/Footsteps in the sands of time', footprints which will be erased by the next tide. We are aware with Virgil that 'irretrievable time is flying'. In our own century W. H. Auden, haunted by the experience of two wars, was to cry out:

> O let not Time deceive you,
> Where Justice naked is,
> Time watches from the shadow
> And coughs when you would kiss.
> In headaches and in worry
> Vaguely life leaks away,
> And Time will have his fancy
> Tomorrow or today.

What is this fear of dying? Is it not compounded of all our fears? And is it not *fear* which ultimately has to be exorcised by ritual? Lock any one of us in a darkened room and, left alone, completely alone, even for a day, our hidden fears will come out from under their stones: the fear of failure; the fear that love will not last and that, in the end, we shall be rejected; the fear that we may lose our job or fail to pay the mortgage, the rent, the bills; the fear that we have taken on too much, been too ambitious, too much the high

60

flyer; the fear that we may do something irrational which will ruin our lives or our careers; or the fear that some skeleton we had locked away will come tumbling out of its cupboard. We think that we are in control of our lives until, suddenly, something takes hold of us and sends us sprawling; the unconscious trips up the conscious self.

In addition there are those atavistic fears, far more common than we realize or even care to admit, such as fear of the dark, of the unexpected, of small animals and insects. Some live in terror of being mugged, or of being stranded in an unknown place (a situation which crops up regularly in dreams). Many of these fears are projections of our own *shadow* side, those aspects of our natures which all too often we prefer to ignore and even will not admit exist. Such hidden fears as these, and what the *shadow* side has to teach us, are uncovered only through analysis or meditation. A fear of heights, for example, may be traced back to a childhood experience. Similarly, early experiences of incest, abuse, rape or parental rows; early betrayal by an authority figure (parent, teacher, priest or relative); early experiences of family break-up or moving home; our first sexual fears and failures; all these play their part and contribute to our adult fears. The list is endless and, however mature or successful we may become, all too often these fears lie just beneath the surface, only waiting for an opportunity to manifest themselves. In very successful people there is also, very often, the irrational fear of being found out, of being proved to be a sham, stemming perhaps from some earlier inferiority.

But what do all these fears have in common? Is it not the fear of the unknown, typified by fear of the dark when nothing can be identified or distinguished, when all orientation is lost? It is the fear of not knowing our identity, of having to let go of all that is most familiar and reassuring. It is interesting that the eminent neurologist, Dr Oliver Sacks, admitted in an interview: 'I'm slightly afraid of the dark. I like to be up for the first light. I need the sunrise to remind me that there is a world out there. I think a feeling of death arises in the darkness.' It is the fear of the dark, the fear of that frontier or bourn 'from which no traveller returns . . . the dread of something *after* death'.

It may well be, therefore, that instead of one ritual for dying we need many rituals for those countless small deaths which we experience on our way to physical death: the death of a love or a relationship or of an ambition. Perhaps also we need rituals for ageing as each decade leads into the next and so closer to our moment of departure.

How ancient rituals may be rediscovered and new rituals emerge is the subject of this book, but the most demanding of all rituals are those which are linked to physical death. There are those who, like Elisabeth Kübler-Ross, believe that funerals are meant simply to gratify the needs of the family, relatives and friends, to help them through the various stages of mourning, rather than for the soul of the deceased. The chief difficulty is that in our society today there seems to be a general conspiracy that death has not occurred. Joan King, writing about her husband's death in the *Guardian*, observed:

> Hardest of all was never being allowed to face the truth . . . Even when the final phone call woke me early one morning, the staff nurse merely felt I ought to come in. Peter was by then mercifully unconscious. The jovial doctor who had assured him three days earlier that he would soon be well and strong and off home again was nowhere to be seen. Instead, a doctor I hadn't met before took me through my husband's dossier, listing the endless rounds of blood-tests and X-rays to which he had been subjected and explaining that the next move would be a biopsy. When I tried to tell him that my husband's life was almost over, he brushed my pessimism aside. An hour later Peter died. Since when, silence. No GP, no district nurse, nothing. Yet within the limits of their knowledge and skill the doctors and nurses almost certainly did their best for my husband. What they weren't prepared to accept was that he was a brave, intelligent human being who had a right to know he was dying.

As Lily Pincus observed in *Death and the Family*, we lack those rites of passage which allow for psychological transition, to help the dying confront their own passing, and to assist the bereaved to adjust to their new status and to those around them. Our society does not provide a climate in which grief and mourning are accepted and supported – although here it must be added that the

AIDS crisis is teaching a whole generation a compassionate and creative approach to dying and death. We *need* to mourn a loss and if this is not made possible then we are likely to suffer either psychologically or physically or both. 'Death is indeed a fearful piece of brutality,' wrote Jung in his memoirs. 'There is no sense in pretending otherwise. It is brutal not only as a physical event but far more so psychically: a human being is torn away from us, and what remains is the icy stillness of death.'

It often happens that a person who has lost someone has an accident after a funeral. Sometimes they slip and badly bruise themselves and the sheer physical pain takes their mind off the psychical pain; or, as is frequent, they step out in front of a passing lorry or car. We all know people who, after a bereavement, say, 'I don't want to go on living.' Whatever the explanation, there is a very strong death wish at work. This is especially the case if we lose someone with whom we have lived closely, for the simple reason that an enormous amount of psychic energy goes into the making of such a relationship and when suddenly it is interrupted, cut off, the energy flows back into us and has nowhere to go.

Often it erupts in the form of anger towards God, towards fate or other people, hence the savage disputes over wills. Faced with the brutality of death and its inevitability, it is not surprising that the desire for immortality should prove to be such a basic need, recurring in all cultures and at all periods of history. We are unwilling to believe that life ends in death either for ourselves or for our friends. And this desire often takes bizarre and even comic forms. I am reminded of Augustus Hare's account in his memoirs of the great tomb of the Duke of Hamilton at Hamilton Palace, which the Duke had built for himself, his son, his grandson, and his nine predecessors. 'What a grand sight it will be,' said the Duke, 'when the twelve Dukes of Hamilton rise together at the Resurrection!' The last drive he took was to purchase spices for his own embalming. He lies buried inside the sarcophogus of an Egyptian queen which he brought especially from Thebes. Frequently he would lie down inside it to see how it fitted. When he was dying, however, he was so haunted by the idea that his body might be too long to go inside the queen that his last words were, 'Double me up! Double me up!' After he was dead, says Augustus

Hare, no amount of doubling up would get him into the mummy case and so they had to cut off his feet to do it!

Most religions encompass, in one form or another, ideas of resurrection or spiritual longevity. We can see it expressed in a rich variety of ways in many different cultures. The egg, for example, is to be found throughout the world in connection with death and the idea of resurrection and rebirth. According to Vedic writings the cosmic egg has a spirit dwelling within it which will be born, die and be born again. Prajapati is described in Hindu mythology as forming the egg and then appearing from it himself. Brahma does likewise, and there are parallels in the ancient legend of Thoth and Ra, while Egyptian pictures of Osiris (the resurrected corn god) show him returning to life rising up from the shell of an egg. It is not surprising, therefore, that the egg became the symbol of resurrection for the Christian church and that it was incorporated into Easter rituals. Painted wooden eggs would also be laid on graves at Easter especially in the Orthodox Church, and these rites may well have had their origin in early Greek votive offerings from the dead. Thus we find many statues of Dionysus in Boetian tombs, clasping an egg. A cup containing five eggs, dated to the late fifth century BC, was found in a tomb on Rhodes. Such offerings, suggests Venetia Newell in her authoritative study, *An Egg At Easter*, may have been connected with the Orphic Mysteries in which eggs were regarded as sacred objects. Even in England, as in Switzerland, eggs have been found in tombs. So many examples from so many different cultures demonstrate the recurring myth of the cosmic egg to be a powerful archetype.

In the Middle Ages the three officiating priests at the Easter mass would take eggs (usually ostrich) up to the altar and lay them on it, as they exchanged the greeting 'Christ is Risen!' An egg was also laid in the representation of the tomb to symbolize Christ. And I remember one Easter Saturday on Rhode Island when I was invited to join in the painting of hard-boiled eggs in their shells for the following day. I became wholly absorbed in the task and found myself painting on one egg the words 'God is a broken egg', whereupon an Episcopalian who was present became very angry, assuming that I was being flippant and irreverent. But of course what I had painted, quite intuitively, is both theologically and psychologically sound. Christ, like the egg, has to be broken, like the bread in the eucharist, if He is to be reborn and nourish all who eat. At the psychological and spiritual level it may also be said that for each of us the hard shell of the ego has to be broken if the real self is to emerge.

DEATH, BEREAVEMENT AND RITUAL

While funeral rituals enable those who are bereaved to make a rite of passage, in most religious cultures they are expressly intended for the psychic and spiritual welfare of the departed soul. Thus in *The Tibetan Book of the Dead* we find precise and complex instructions that must be carried out on behalf of the deceased. Such rituals are to be found in other cultures and traditions, aimed at helping the departing spirits to continue on their journey. In Europe, windows and doors would be opened or a tile removed from the roof to let the spirit out, or mirrors would be covered lest the soul be distracted and lose its way. In some mountainous parts of Japan still, according to Carmen Blacker, paths will be cut in the long grass to enable spirits to make their way more easily from their mountain realm to their old homes. Bonfires on the tops of hills would be lit for the same reason.

In his book *The Tibetan Book of Living and Dying*, Sogyal Rinpoche describes how when he first came to the West in 1970:

> ... what disturbed me deeply, and has continued to disturb me, is the almost complete lack of spiritual help for the dying that exists in modern culture ... I have been told many stories of people dying alone and in great distress and disillusion in the West without any spiritual help ... Wherever I go in the West, I am struck by the great mental suffering that arises from the fear of dying, whether or not this fear is acknowledged. In Tibet it was a natural response to pray for the dying and to give them spiritual care; in the West the only spiritual attention that the majority pay to the dying is to go to their funeral.

At the moment of their greatest vulnerability, he remarks, people are abandoned and left almost totally without support or insight.

This is a tragic and humiliating state of affairs, which must change. All of the modern world's pretensions to power and success will ring hollow, he concludes, until everyone in our culture can die with some measure of true peace, and until some measure is taken to ensure that this is possible.

In shamanistic culture, the shamans have always been aware of the journey to be undertaken by the soul after death, which is why they spend time with a person who is dying, so that they might counsel them and calm their fears about what awaits them on the other side. Few clergy today take such time in preparing the dying in this manner. I know of one remarkable exception, Metropolitan Anthony Bloom of the Russian Orthodox Church in London. I recall his account, typical of him, of visiting one of his parishioners, a man of forty, married with children, at the peak of his career, and lying in hospital dying of cancer. Metropolitan Anthony visited him daily, spending many hours at his bedside, guiding him through the journey of such questions as 'Why me?' and the resulting bitterness. On the last day of his life, as he lay on his bed, an emaciated figure with large eyes, he looked up smiling at Father Anthony and said with great serenity and joy, 'Oh, Father! It is only now, as I am dying, that I feel I am really beginning to live!'

To the Saxon Wicca, who, like Buddhists and Hindus, believed in reincarnation, death symbolized the end of a learning period, so that for them a funeral was not a wake but an awakening. Sorrow, they believed, is only a symptom of selfishness on our part. We are sorry for ourselves that we have been left behind without the love of those dearest to us. St Bernard of Clairvaux, writing in the twelfth century, expressed most poignantly the pain we all feel on such occasions. Speaking of the death of a member of the community, he wrote: 'It is not over our brother that we must weep, it is over me, over all of you and over this house: there is no other sadness for us than to be deprived of his advice and example; but for our brother death is an opening on joy and gaiety for eternity.' In his famous Sermon 26 on *The Song of Songs* we also find his lamentation for his own brother Gerard; it is a lament not so much for Gerard's passing but for Bernard's existence henceforth without him. 'I weep because of you, not over you ... Our love had created between us a presence, one to the other. In truth we were of one heart, one spirit; between us there was more than community of blood, there was an unity of soul.'

One of the most haunting of all arias which expresses this profound sense of loss is that of Orpheus in Gluck's opera, *Orfé*: '*Che faro senza Eurydice?*' – 'What shall I do without Eurydice? Thou art gone, O Eurydice! Eurydice! Where can I go without my beloved? What will I do, where can I go, what will I do without my love?' Many passages in literature echo such feelings as we cry out for those whom we have lost:

> Parthenophil is lost and I should see him:
> For he is like to something I should remember,
> A great while since, a long time ago.

One of the earliest laments is from the ancient Sumerian epic, *Gilgamesh*:

> I weep for Enkidu, my friend . . .
> O Enkidu, my brother,
> You were the axe at my side . . .
> O my younger brother, Enkidu, my dearest friend,
> What is this sleep which holds you now?
> You are lost in the dark and cannot hear me.

And so it is that Gilgamesh sets forth on his last great journey in search of the secret of immortality. After many difficulties he crosses through mountains and over oceans and comes finally to Utnapishtim, who asks him, 'If you are Gilgamesh, why are your cheeks so starved and your face drawn? Why is despair in your heart and your face like the face of one who has made a long journey? Why do you come here, wandering over the wilderness in search of the wind?' And Gilgamesh replies, 'My friend, my younger brother, who was very dear to me and who endured dangers beside me, Enkidu, my brother, whom I loved, the end of mortality has overtaken him. I wept for him seven days and seven nights until the worms fastened on him. Because of my brother I am afraid of death. His fate lies heavy upon me. How can I be silent, how can I rest? He is dust and I shall die also and be laid in the earth for ever.'

It is no wonder that, faced with such grief, we should require rituals which will enable us to come to terms with it. The great death rituals enable the bereaved to return to life and to adjust to the absence of the loved one and, at the same time, enable the soul of the deceased to go on its way. Even on a psychological level we have to learn how to let go of the one who has died. In the Saxon Wicca ritual *Crossing the Bridge at Death* the priest says these words: 'We gather here to say farewell to a friend who must travel far. There is a reason for being here in this world and this life. There is a reason for leaving when the purposes of this life are done. The soul must journey beyond to pause, to rest, to wait for those who are loved. For the world beyond is a land of eternal summer and of joy, far from the cares of this world, with happiness and youth anew.' The priest then places on top of the coffin three evergreen boughs and continues: 'As the evergreen does grow and prosper both in summer and winter, year after year, so also does the soul continue from life to life, growing ever stronger, wiser and richer.'

I recall having to take the funeral of Kathleen Lomax in the tiny hamlet of Knill in Herefordshire. She was one of the first women students at Cambridge, and had worked all her life in the research laboratories of the Milk Marketing Board. On her retirement she came to live in a black and white Tudor cottage nearby. Kathleen had very bad arthritis as well as Parkinson's disease. She was in her mid-eighties and people worried about her living alone, but I argued that this was what she wanted. She used to read four or five books a week, was intensely interested in other people, and kept her cottage and garden in immaculate condition. Always she would insist on providing a three-course lunch which she prepared and cooked herself, followed afterwards by coffee in her drawing room. Because of her condition everything took her much longer to do than it would most people, but she was a perfectionist. I loved her company and became a close friend. Twelve days before she died, she was taken to hospital with a haemorrhage and it was clear that she would not return. It so happened that I was able to be with her every day and on the last day I stayed with her for twelve hours. After her death I asked some of her neighbours to cut down boughs of autumn branches from the woods above her cottage. I also asked them to go and collect from her home that season's fruit which she had just bottled, as well as the wooden boxes full of that autumn's apples which she had gathered and stored away for the winter, each apple nestling in a circle of paper. We also collected some of the books which she herself had bound in leather before the Parkinson's had taken hold. 'Let us deck the church as for a harvest festival!' I said, 'For it is to be a celebration of the harvesting of Kathleen's life.' And so it was, with a special liturgy created for the occasion.

Today, when many do not want a formal religious ceremony, the idea of creating one's own ceremony is more familiar. While perhaps a solemn requiem mass, especially in a magnificent cathedral or church, cannot be equalled for its solemnity and sense of the soul going forth to meet its maker, the simplicity of a Quaker funeral service is likely to appeal more as a pattern. Here, everyone sits, sharing a silence which is interrupted at intervals by someone sharing a particular memory so that, slowly, a portrait is built up of the departed person, composed of many memories. Such a ceremony conveys a very real sense of people coming together to remember with affection and also to let go.

We may create rituals for a funeral but we have none for the continuing sense of loss during a bereavement, which may last one or two years or even longer. There are many instances in which an individual never really comes to terms with the loss of a partner or a child. People who are bereaved will often visit the grave regularly and in some cases this can become obsessive. One mother, whose daughter died at the age of seven, continues to visit her grave twice a year, on the anniversaries of her birthday and of her death. On each visit she carries red roses – one for each year of her daughter's life had she gone on living. This past year it meant fourteen roses and, as she said, it was becoming 'more than I can afford'. Quite clearly, apart from the cost, she is finding the bereavement 'more than she can afford', being unable to let go of her grief and therefore of her daughter. There is also something very revealing and negative about the fact of 'severed' roses. Perhaps if she can be encouraged to plant a rose tree and to think of her daughter as released into a new life, her own life, then slowly she may be able to let go, as she would have had to let go of her daughter once she had grown up and left home had she lived.

Visits to the graveside are not always obsessive or retrogressive. In Italy and other Mediterranean countries one can observe whole families going to the cemetery on a Sunday, as an outing, to place fresh flowers on a grave, laughing and chatting and even enjoying a picnic. Grief has to be expressed, not only in tears, but also creatively. I think often of 'Phyll's garden' in the tiny village churchyard of East Dean in Sussex, England, where Phyll, the wife of the playwright Christopher Fry, lies buried. Years before, when I first visited him there, he took me up to his study and looking out of the window said, 'Do you see the village church on the hill over there? And do you see that corner of the churchyard? That's where Phyll and I are to be buried when the time comes. We have booked our patch of ground.' When Phyll died, unexpectedly, Christopher Fry turned that patch of ground into a garden in memory of Phyll. He had a large stone set up at the head, like a bedhead, and carved on it are her name, the date of her birth and of her death; alongside is Christopher Fry's name, his date of birth and a blank left for the date of his death. In the small garden he has planted many shrubs and flowers, set up a bird bath and, to one side, a stone seat. Here he can sit and look across the valley to his study window. Often when friends visit him, he will say, 'Shall we go up and look at Phyll's garden?'

In his memoirs Carl Jung describes how he could hardly have survived his wife's death if he had not constantly worked at his stone carving. In 1957 he wrote, 'Everything that I have written this year and last year has grown out of the stone sculptures I did after my wife's death. The close of her life, the end, and what it made me realise, wrenched me violently out of myself. It cost me a great deal to regain my footing, and contact with stone helped me.'

Of all bereavements the most painful is that of a mother who loses her child, whether as a youngster or as an adult. The bonding of mother and child that occurs during the nine months of pregnancy is more intimate and intense than that of any other relationship. One woman, a Quaker, sent me a copy of a liturgy which she created out of her grief at the sudden and unexpected death of her grown-up daughter. She wrote it when, as she describes it, 'I was in the depths. It worked and continues to work for me. How lost and desperate everyone is.' Entitled *A Simple Ritual for Coming*

Alive (the title itself conveys vividly the essence of the experience of
working through a bereavement when, indeed, something in one's
own self dies), it begins with certain instructions: 'Music: the
opening bars of Mozart's *Requiem* which die away. Silence. A
desolate landscape of rocks, ruins, and tree skeletons under snow in
a grey twilight. The wind provides a chorus.' These images which
set the scene describe strikingly her own feelings – desolate, ruined,
skeletal, in a grey twilight. The images begin to accumulate:

Chorus:	This is Death's time.
	The sun has fallen out of the sky.
	Darkness and cold pervade the earth.
	Darkness follows darkness,
	Cold grows upon cold.
	Out of a leaden sky
	Falls the stilling snow.
	It blurs and smothers all forms,
	Smudges the last pale glow from fallen leaves,
	Dulls the last sounds.
	Immaculate snow, skeletal trees
	In a grey twilight
	Are all that remain in the perpetual silence.
First Voice:	Perpetual silence.
	It was always like this.
	A remote sun arose on the edge of the world,
	A brief gesture of faint yellow across the grey.
	And sank once more.
	No eyes reflected the beginning.
Chorus:	'In the beginning God created ...' and recreates
	Out of the stillness, cold, darkness and death.

First Voice: 'I am the Light.'

Chorus: 'Let there be Light, for ever and
                                  ever, Amen.'

First Voice: And I am the dark, stillness and
                                  cold.
                                  Stay with me. Submit.
                                  Accept the totality without fear.
                                  What do you fear?

Chorus: We fear what we do not understand,
                                  What we cannot see,
                                  What threatens our life.

First Voice: I am the Life, the Truth, and the
                                  Way.
                                  I am totality.
                                  I am in All
                                  All is in me.

Second Voice: I make an act of faith.
                                  I take this seed of my life,
                                  I go into the darkness, into the snow
                                  And delve a shallow grave
                                  In the frozen earth.
                                  I plant this seed, my life.

Chorus: This is the time of Advent.
                                  The Eternal Seed
                                  Still in its Mother Earth,
                                  Will come again with the Sun
                                  And renew All Life.

Second Voice: Let my life be His Life, O Tao,
                                  Splendid, Generous Burgeoning
                                  World
                                  In all its Beautiful Intricacy and
                                  Breadth.

Chorus and Voices Together: Eternal, Everchanging,
                                     All Pervading,
                                     We prostrate ourselves before You
                                     On this First Day.

Light grows in intensity, through the spectrum: first blue, purple, red, orange, yellow, then white, to reveal the garments of the chorus covered with living flowers, leaves and grass, birds upon their shoulders and on their heads. Music grows, made up of birdsong, cloud, wind in the trees and the stars.

In reading such a liturgy it is important to remember that every voice in it is also the voice of the person who wrote it, just as in a dream we are every character and situation in that dream, so that in analysing such a dream or piece of work we need to examine it from the point of view of each character within it. Each one of us is a company of many selves, and these selves are often acting in contradiction of each other, causing conflict and pain to our conscious selves, for we are, most of us, relatively unacquainted with these hidden players and their roles. 'Whether we will it or not, our inner characters are constantly seeking a stage on which to play out their tragedies or comedies. Moreover, it is the inner world with its repeating repertory that determines most of what happens to us in the external world.' It is revealing that the author of this liturgy so strongly felt the need to cast it in a dramatic form, as something to be acted out if only on the stage of her inner being. Her statement that 'it continues still to work for me' reminds us also of another important element of ritual, that of repetition. Once the ritual has emerged from the depths of our being, it can be repeated many times in memory, until we have worked through our pain, loss, grief, celebration or thanksgiving.

Grief is the hardest thing of which to let go. As the Rinpoche remarks in Andrew Harvey's *A Journey in Ladakh*, 'Be sad, but not too sad. Grieve, but do not become absorbed in your grief. You cannot change what you have done. But you can change what you will become. Remember that somewhere you are free already. Buddha. Draw from that. Live in that hope.'

'It is hard,' observes Andrew Harvey.

'It is the hardest thing,' replies the Rinpoche. 'That is why you must practice. The Self wants sometimes to give up, to abandon itself to despair. Despair is one of the last houses of the ego. And that house too has to be burnt down. We must abide in nothing and nowhere.'

There are occasions when the bereaved person is unable to be present at the funeral and does not really have the opportunity to work through their loss. On such occasions I sometimes use the bereavement ritual described in the Exercises section, which enables everyone in the group to share in their individual experience of loss.

I first tried it with a group of about fifty nuns in London who had assembled from different parts of the world for their annual chapter. They stood in a circle in their spacious chapel suspended from the roof of which was a pyx containing the blessed sacrament. On the floor, in the centre, was a circular basket filled with balls of wool, each ball a different colour. Each person present was asked to think of someone they knew who had died, and then to take one of the balls of wool from the central basket, choosing the colour that reminded them of that person. When everyone had selected a ball of wool and returned to their place in the circle, each was asked to thread a few inches of wool around the finger of one hand, thus tethering the wool, and then to throw the ball with the other hand towards someone on the other side of the circle towards whom they felt drawn or in sympathy. Slowly the balls of wool began to fly back and forth, the coloured threads crossing and recrossing, until a giant tapestry was being woven by the group. As the action gathered momentum the nuns began singing, quite spontaneously, a hymn 'For all the saints who from their labours rest'.

Finally the tapestry was so heavy that it began to sag. At this point I handed a pair of scissors to an African nun, who had asked if she might watch, and invited her to go slowly round the circle cutting off the threads of wool attached to each person's hand, leaving each with just a few inches of coloured wool – like the memory of all those who had died. Indeed, what they had discovered was that in grieving for one particular person they had ended up in sharing in each other's grief for all those who had died. As the threads were severed one by one, the tapestry began to subside to the floor. I waited to see what would happen. From now on the exercise was wide open to their response. At the end, one of the younger nuns stepped forward and began to gather up the tapestry into a large bundle and place it in the circular basket. Finally she lifted the basket up towards the blessed sacrament overhead in the pyx, at which moment the nuns burst into a joyous singing of 'Sanctus! Sanctus! Sanctus!'

In the discussion which followed, one of the nuns described how she had been in Australia when a very close friend had died, and she had been unable to attend the funeral. Only now, through this ritual, had she been able to attend the funeral. Only now, through this ritual, had she been able to work through her grief and finally say farewell. A word of warning however! This ritual resolved itself in so harmonious a way because all those present were united by a common way of life and belief and discipline. With a group from varying backgrounds it is more difficult. Once, after I had described the above incident at a lecture I was giving, I was approached by a woman who told me that she led workshops in bereavement and that she was now going to use this in her workshops. I was struck speechless, because it is an exercise that requires handling with skill and sensitivity.

In general our society has lost touch with the idea of a continuing relationship with the departed. In the Roman Catholic Church there are two very important feasts which are also celebrated by some Anglicans and Episcopalians: those of All Souls and of All Saints. Winter is a time of dying, when the daylight shrinks. It is not surprising therefore that in the eighth century, the Church in the West should have created the Feast of All Saints at the onset of winter, grafting it upon a more ancient ceremony, the Druidical feast of Saman, Lord of Death. On the night of his feast it was believed that witches and ghosts were abroad and that wicked souls escaped from hell — hence the lighting of Hallowe'en bonfires and lanterns as a protection in the surrounding darkness. Darkness is something which our ancestors understood more vividly than do we. They went to bed with the setting of the sun and they rose with the dawn. Beeswax candles were costly and burned more quickly than modern candles. One can easily imagine a church or cathedral deep in shadow on a winter's morning with only the flickering of two candles reflected in the gilt and brocade of the priest's vestments, and the blessed sacrament in its monstrance rising like the sun itself.

Darkness is frightening to a child and also, as we have seen, to many adults. The approach of winter in the western hemisphere affects people, especially the elderly, psychosomatically. Darkness obliterates all known landmarks, removing all sense of identity. The ancient Feast of All Saints marks the edge of this darkness. It speaks to us of the massive power of evil not only 'out there' but all about us and within us. And so at the edge of the winter darkness the faithful would light their candles of prayer, knowing that they were not alone but encompassed about on every side by a mighty gathering of saints, as is expressed in the Office for the Feast of All Saints: 'What you have come to is Mount Sion, the City of the Living God, the heavenly Jerusalem, where the millions of living angels have gathered for the festival with the whole Church in which everyone is a firstborn son and a citizen of heaven.'

Similarly in Japan we find that certain times of the year are set aside for remembering those who have died, and for the recall of ancestral spirits to their ancestral homes: the Festival of the New Year and the Festival of Bon. This latter occurs about the middle of August and on the last evening of the festival there is the ritual of *tor-nagashi*, when floating lanterns are launched upon the waters of the great lake at Matsue. Each lantern has the family name written on one side and on the other a valedictory prayer. Thousands of these flickering lanterns float slowly across the waters like a great company of spirits sailing into the impenetrable darkness.

A comparable ritual is held each year in Rio de Janeiro on New Year's Eve by the devotees of Macumba, a matriarchal religion which has been described as the Brazilian Voodoo, and is a powerful cult based on old beliefs and pagan rites, dominated by priestesses. The ritual celebrates the death of the old year and the birth of the new. As many as a million people will gather on the beach at Copabanca to throw white flowers out to sea to propitiate Iemanja, the goddess of the sea. They also send her presents: cigars, fruit, wine – and these gifts are arranged in little boats fashioned from wood and straw, in the middle of which is a candle, and on one side the owner's name. As midnight approaches everyone moves down to the water's edge. The candles in the small boats are lit and then, on the stroke of midnight, the thousands of small vessels are launched upon the ocean, and white flowers hurled through the air until the sea is carpeted.

It is interesting to compare these two rituals with an account by Richard Chadwick of a funeral at the London Lighthouse, the first residential and day-care centre in Britain for the growing number of women and men affected by HIV. Its principal aim is to 'guide people safely home', by offering an integral range of services, to care for people from the initial diagnosis of HIV infection through to providing a loving environment where the terminally ill can die with dignity. Eduardo's lover, Peter, had died some months before but Eduardo had not been able to find a place where he could say goodbye in a way that he wanted. Then, after a weekend workshop, he realized that that place was in fact the Lighthouse community, surrounded by the love and support of his brothers and sisters there.

> So he asked that we should go with him to Shoreham and scatter Peter's ashes. We stood together at the end of the harbour wall, each of us carrying a flower and a memory of a loved one with us. When Eduardo felt ready we gathered round him and watched in silence as he poured Peter's ashes over the water, saying farewell to his friend. Nothing was rushed and Eduardo was safe with us to feel all he needed to. We then threw in our flowers to accompany Peter out to sea, speaking the names of other loved ones as we did so. We sang 'Jerusalem', Peter's favourite hymn. I remember us all feeling very close. That was the first glimpse I had that the whole-hearted recognition of death was not the end but the beginning of living our lives with meaning. Being there was part of the meaning. To live well we have to discover how to die well, and the funeral was part of that process.

To live well we have to discover how to die well. Marie Mathias, at the age of ninety, wrote to me, 'James, I need you to teach me how to die well.' To die well is indeed a great achievement.

Since I am coming to that holy room
Where, with Thy quire of Saints for evermore
I shall be made Thy Music; as I come
I tune the instrument here at the door,
And what I must do then, think here before.

John Donne

The elderly often know when they are going to die and, in many instances, even set their own clock. Richard Lamerton describes an elderly Polish teacher who, when told that another course of treatment for cancer might lengthen her life a little, replied, 'I think I would prefer to be left in peace. I am not afraid to die. And I thank you very much for giving me this warning, for taking the first step in preparing me for the long journey ahead.' Six weeks later she died peacefully. Dying is setting forth upon a journey, a voyage of discovery. Not to let someone know that they are dying, not to be able to share with them the experience, to pretend, to lie, is to deprive a human being of perhaps the most crucial phase of their living.

I remember a friend, Aileen Dance, who was in her eighties when she fell and broke her hip, and was taken to a London hospital. She knew that she would never be allowed to return to her flat and that she would have to live in a nursing home, which she did not want. 'Why can't they give me something to end it all?' she said. In reply I quoted to her from *King Lear*, 'We must endure our going hence.' Recognizing the quotation (she had been a Shakespearean actress with the company of Sir Frank Benson), she smiled broadly, clutching my hand, and accepting what lay ahead. Although I was directing a production at the time, I used to go each evening to spend an hour with her. One day she said, 'I know that when the time comes I shall open my eyes and you will be there.' This is exactly what happened. On the last day of her life the hospital telephoned to tell me that she was failing and that I should go at once. She lay on her bed, thin, emaciated, yellow, her eyes closed. The matron approached her, bent down and then, quite inexplicably, shouted in her ear, 'Mrs Dance, you have a visitor.' Her eyes still closed, there came from Aileen Dance a great bellow: 'GO AWAY!' worthy of Frank Benson and every Victorian actor! The matron withdrew, and as I approached she opened her eyes and looked up at me. Those eyes were so alert, full of intelligence and humour and love. For a few moments we gazed at each other and then she closed her eyes once more. A few hours later she was dead. I experienced then in those moments, as she was dying, the luminosity of the spirit. I learned also on other visits to her the importance of just *being* with a person who is dying. Often she would be in a coma, not responding to any outside stimulus. Yet sitting there, holding her hand, meditating, I would sometimes say something quietly to her, and her grip would respond, acknowledging what was said. It is my intuition that those who are unconscious are so only on the superficial level, that deep down, wherever the psyche is, there is much happening.

We tend to think of rituals as being for the departed rather than for the dying, but the dying need rituals also. For those who have a particular religious discipline there are existing last rites, but what is to be done for the great majority of people who have no specific religious beliefs? It is here that Sogyal Rinpoche's book, *The Tibetan Book of Living and Dying* is of major importance. At the close of the book, he writes:

> More than anything, I pray that the book I have written could contribute in some small way to help awaken as many people as possible to the urgency of the need for spiritual transformation, and the urgency of the need to be responsible for ourselves and others. We are all potential buddhas, and we all desire to live in peace and die in peace . . . Knowledge about death, about how to help the dying, and about the spiritual nature of death and dying should be made available to all levels of society; it should be taught in depth and with real imagination in schools and colleges and universities of all kinds; and especially and most important, it should be available in teaching hospitals to nurses and doctors who will look after the dying and who have so much responsibility towards them.

We need a quiet revolution in the whole way we look at death and care for the dying, and in consequence at the whole way we look at life and care for the living. In the meantime each one of us who visits the dying must be open and responsive to ways in which we can assist. What does the dying person most want and need? It may call for gentle skills in counselling, being alert to the smallest hint, to discover this. We have but to let people talk and we will learn. It may be that the dying want to see certain people, to say goodbye, or to make reconciliation with those from whom they have been parted. There is usually a desire to see things in order, to make a will, to plan their own funeral service. It is very important that people be gently invited to talk about such things, and planning one's own service is often a creative way of coming to terms with the reality of letting go, of saying goodbye, and of reviewing one's life. I had one friend in her seventies, who had a great love of music, and who loved the lines of John Donne quoted above. Often we would say them together:

> Since I am coming to that holy room
> Where with Thy quire of Saints for evermore
> I shall be made Thy Music; as I come
> I tune the instrument here at the door,
> And what I shall do then, think here before.

Everything will depend upon the individual. Some may want to revisit certain places that have a resonance for them. Such journeys are always in the nature of a pilgrimage and those who accompany them on such a journey will need to be sensitive to when it is time to talk and when to be silent. The dying person may want to sit or lie under a tree, gazing up into its branches, or be allowed to sit out, well wrapped up, if only for a few moments, under the stars, sensing the mightiness of the universe. They may desire to go to a last concert, or listen to music on tapes. I think of one man who devoted the last months of his life, as he died of cancer, to listening to and studying the last quartets of Beethoven.

A regular visitor might introduce a ritual of lighting a candle or a night-light for the duration of a visit, and just sit quietly gazing at its flame. The gentle movement of the flame, like a living presence, can have a very calming and healing effect. Sometimes the dying person may like to be helped to create a collage of snapshots, representing their journey through life. Often a handshake, an embrace, a kiss, can assume a ritualistic importance as well as the simple reassurance that someone cares. Each of these gestures can be perfunctory or it can be powerfully expressive, beyond the reach of words. With the very sick, as with the dying, such tactile contact is very important. A woman friend of mine, visiting a young man dying of AIDS, who had been blinded by the disease, used always to massage his feet, and he would weep.

One of the most difficult tasks for the dying, perhaps most of all for the elderly, is learning how to let go and just *be*, so that they can in the fullness of time, like a ripening apple from the tree, let go. All too often the elderly cling tenaciously to life and power. If we are to die well we have to start learning *now* how to let go of each moment. But it is not enough to know these things intellectually, one must learn them experientially. The great strength of ritual, when it is performed with the totality of our being, is that we gain insights on an intuitive rather than an intellectual level. This is why ritual can effect changes which analysis cannot always achieve; and even within analysis it is the *experience* of a dream, as its full meaning is slowly absorbed, rather than a cerebral analysis of its contents, which can prove transforming.

It is in the nature of ritual to lead one across the threshold of liminality into an experience of gnosis, of insight. I was reminded of this when leading a workshop on the Shakers, that remarkable sect which split off from the Quakers (they came to be known as the Shaking Quakers) and who with their leader Ann Lee, set sail from England and settled in America just over 250 years ago. I set out to recreate one of their meetings for worship which would employ a great deal of physical movement and dance, songs, hymns, shouts, cries and glossalia. Their ecstatic meetings would go on for hours, breaking the barriers of time and fatigue, and, rather in the manner of Gurdjieff's famous dances, release new sources of energy. The meetings would usually commence with everyone walking swiftly across the floor of the meeting house, each worshipper following a different path, each intent upon her or his journey, criss-crossing one another but never colliding. This pattern would then be succeeded by a new one which consisted of each person, as they passed another, giving that person a shove in the chest which would set them spinning, until eventually the whole assembly would be spinning like tops. Thereafter the movement would break up into a variety of patterns, of jumping, rolling, tumbling and so on. At the end of the day's workshop we performed the meeting for worship and afterwards sat down to discuss the experience. One of the performers, Cynthia O'Brien, a physiotherapist who worked at the local hospice, spoke at length about what she had learned from this experience of being shoved and then going into the whirling movement. Normally, in every-day life, she remarked, if someone shoves us our response will be to tense up and hit back. In the Shaker ritual, however, one does not resist but goes with the shove, allowing it to turn one around. In yielding to this thrust and going into a spin, the body is led into other sequences of movement, each flowing out from the other. It is all very Zen-like, reminiscent of the teachings of Lao Tzu who describes how when water (river or stream) meets an obstacle such as a rock, instead of hurling itself against the rock, as we tend to do when we hit an obstacle, flows round it, dividing itself in two and then continuing on the other side with renewed force, having first absorbed the obstacle, converting the rock into an island. This movement of push and yield is central to the Shaker philosophy as expressed in the words of the Shaker hymn 'Simple Gifts' (which was not composed by Aaron Copland though he used the melody to great effect in *Appalachian Spring*, and which was further adapted by Sidney Carter for his hymn, 'The Lord of the Dance'):

> 'Tis the gift to be simple,
> 'Tis the gift to be free,
> 'Tis the gift to come down,
> Where we ought to be.
>
> And when we come round right
> In the place just right
> 'Twill be in the valley
> Of love and delight.
>
> To turn, turn
> Will be our delight,
> Till by turning, turning,
> We come round right!

Cynthia O'Brien, in her work with the dying, had also observed that those who had the most difficult deaths were always those people who found it difficult in life to yield, while those who died serenely were the ones who had learned how to be flexible,

> To go with the drift of things,
> To yield with a grace to reason,
> To accept the end of a love or a season.
>   Robert Frost

This particular insight, which I also experienced during this recreation of a Shaker meeting for worship, was achieved by *doing*, by the movement itself, not through any words. My description here is not the same, for, reduced to words, it is merely information, and not the experience itself. A true ritual will always take one beyond and deeper than words, to the very source of words, for words are but symbols of a deeper reality. Once I attended, by invitation, a Sufi meeting for worship in London, where the circular Sufi dances are performed. I arrived an hour early in order to 'centre down'. Shortly before the ceremony was about to commence I opened my notebook in readiness so that I might quietly record my impressions. Very gently, one of the community who was not dancing leaned forward without saying anything and removed the notebook, implying by this gesture: just experience it! This I did, and surrendered myself to the ancient wisdom of those powerful ritual movements.

To live well we have to discover how to die well. At the centre to which each of us has to return, is the need to mourn the passing of each of our many selves. As Robert Bly points out in his book *Iron John*, when Job covered himself with ashes it was his way of saying that the earlier, comfortable Job was dead, and that the living Job mourned the dead Job. We all have occasions to grieve and we all need to be guided through such experiences of loss if we are to grow: As Robert Frost says:

> The question that he frames in all but words
> Is what to make of a diminished thing.

In order to cross such frontiers we need new rituals, or to rediscover ancient rituals.

VIII

The Making of a Ritual

Society in the West has a need to rediscover the art of celebration. Even the simplest meal can take on the aspect and reality of a ritual. A ritual has three stages: the preparation, the event and the conclusion. Thus the preparation of food gives us an opportunity to reflect on those for whom it is being done. We can choose to throw a meal together slap-bang-dash, racing against time (which never does save time) or we can concentrate upon each stage of the preparation, in a Zen-like awareness of the present moment, not resenting the task but identifying with it, wholly focusing on the physical activity and inwardly making it an offering for our guests. Similarly the way we choose to set and lay the table, however simply, continues our reflection on those who are coming to spend time with us and break bread. We are in danger of losing touch with simple rituals of welcome and homecoming and farewell.

The second stage of the meal may be prefaced by a linking of hands around the table and sharing a moment of silence, some lines of poetry, or a simple grace, but without pretension or pomposity! Such a moment, if kept simple and spontaneous, heightens the sense of occasion and the feeling that the breaking of bread is a symbol of giving to one another. The table itself is a symbol of such sharing, especially if it is a round table. A round table brings people together in an equality of sharing which a long table cannot achieve since it imposes a hierarchy of seating: who is to be next to the host or hostess, etc. A round table is not only more conducive to conversation on a practical level but it is also the most democratic way of eating together. We are reminded of the Round Table of King Arthur, itself a mandala. Where a large number of people have to be fed then a series of round tables will enable those present to form smaller communities within the larger community of the occasion.

Finally, when the guests have left there is an opportunity to reflect upon the sharing of such an occasion. Each encounter in life is a gift and each supper may prove to be the last.

A ritual involves an offering of one's self: to a deity, to some cause or higher purpose, or to a fellow human being. My mother had a small ritual which always moved me and continues to work upon me in memory and to influence me even though she is dead. Whenever I was staying with her she would place on my desk an egg-cup filled with tiny flowers which she had picked from the garden or hedgerow. Through this recurring ritual she was able to express her love and watchfulness over me.

Many elements go into the making of a ritual for a public occasion and consequently there has to be an overall structure, for it is the rules that frame a ritual. However, as Victor Turner observed, the ritual process must be able to transcend its frame. 'A river needs banks or it will be a dangerous flood, but banks without a river epitomise aridity.' In the execution of a ritual, as in the performance of a work of theatre, the actual performance is liable to transform itself. The rules may frame the performance but the flow of the action and interaction within the frame may lead to unexpected insights and even generate new symbols and meanings which can then be incorporated into subsequent performances. Theodore Jennings, in a paper *On Ritual Knowledge*, has pointed out that one of the reasons rituals change is that they not only transmit ancient knowledge but also assist the discovery of new knowledge. We learn by doing in the same way that we make a path by walking. For this reason it is important, if there is to be experiment and growth in new rituals or the adaptation of old rituals, that there be time for assessment and reassessment, for asking such questions as: Did the planned ritual achieve its goals, and if not, why not? How might it have been clarified, and what new insights gained? It should be obvious, but often is not, that the ancient rituals and liturgies must have evolved in a similar way, by trial and error, guided as much by the needs and desires of a community as by its holy women and men.

It is important within any ritual to be open to the moment, and even within existing liturgies this is possible. I recall celebrating a eucharist in a small Herefordshire church and among the congregation was Becky, aged about nine, who could only communicate through sounds and occasional words. On this particular Sunday, during the prayer of Consecration, she began to cry out, 'Amen! Amen!' Looking up and seeing her shining face, I called back to her, 'Amen, Becky! Amen! Amen! Amen!' She laughed and clapped her hands as together we repeated the word 'Amen!' Everyone in the small congregation who had been pretending not to notice Becky, looked up smiling. Suddenly Becky's interruption was no longer an embarrassment but had been made part of the eucharistic moment.

I recall a similar moment of openness when I was in Paris directing Edwige Feuillère in the French production of Hugh Whitemore's play *The Best of Friends*, and I used to attend the American Episcopal Cathedral on Sundays. On this particular Sunday I observed that the woman in the pew in front of me kept rubbing her back. She preceded me up to the altar rail for communion. It was then that I noticed that the celebrant, Canon Cindy Taylor, a woman priest, bent down and whispered something to the woman who nodded her head and burst into tears. Later when I came to meet Cindy Taylor I asked her what had happened. 'I simply noticed that she was pregnant, and so I asked her if she would like me to pray for her child.' It is this kind of sensitive awareness and compassion in the midst of a formal liturgy which can make of it a living reality. At such a moment the ritual transcends its frame.

Speaking once at St James's Church, Piccadilly, in London, I was asked by the organizer if I would 'do a ritual' for the two or three hundred people assembled. She was quite angry when I declined, saying that I did not know the people there, nor could I see any reason for creating an *ad hoc* ritual. A ritual cannot be thrown together at a moment's notice, but calls for a long and thoughtful preparation by all concerned. Once it is known for whom such a ritual is intended, and what occasion it is to cele-

brate, all who are involved need to discuss and explore the theme
in detail, examining the many possibilities. Once a pattern begins
to emerge, it is important to examine and work through a checklist
like the following.

1. *Numbers*: How many people are going to be involved as participants and how many will be in the position of observers, in
   pews or rows?

2. *Place*: Where is this to take place? Will there be enough room
   for everyone? Will everyone be able to see clearly what is
   happening?

3. *Space*: What kind of setting and space would be best? Is it to be
   out of doors or indoors? If out of doors, is it to be confined to a
   space such as a garden or a courtyard, or spread over a larger
   area, or longer distance? (Obviously those planning the procession and funeral of President Kennedy had many factors to
   consider.) If it is to cover a larger area how is the event to be
   controlled and people moved from one place to another? If the
   event is indoors, is it planned to utilize other spaces such as
   cellars, corridors, balconies, windows, staircases, other rooms?

4. *Time*: When is the ritual to take place? At dawn, midday, dusk,
   sunset, or night? If the last then, like Snout in *A Midsummer
   Night's Dream*, we may need to ask, 'Doth the moon shine that
   night we play the play?' Is it to coincide with a particular time
   of the year such as the Passover, Yom Kippur, the Chinese New
   Year, Christmas, Easter, and so forth. Finally, how long is the
   ritual to last, using time in its other sense: ten minutes or ten
   hours? Time in this sense is very important. Western society
   tends to rush things, and many clergy tend to rattle through a
   liturgy often in a meaningless jumble of words. But a true ritual
   should break through our conventional sense of time. It is
   significant that when people are absorbed they forget time.
   Peter Brook's amazing production of *The Mahabarata* lasted
   nine hours, with two hour-long intervals through the night,
   ending at dawn, yet wherever it was played it was packed out
   night after night. Similarly with the theatre works of Robert
   Wilson. The question ultimately is: how much time *are* WE
   prepared to give?

Time in terms of tempo is also important. What happens when an action is deliberately slowed down, for example? The washing of another person's feet can be either a perfunctory liturgical gesture lasting a few seconds or it can take an hour or longer and become a rich and powerful experience. In music, time is allowed for 'rests', but all too often in Western liturgies there is little or no space for silence in which time can indeed stand still. Words, like actions, need space and time within which to breathe and resonate.

5. *Costume*: What are the participants to wear? What is the function of costume, of liturgical robes, of uniforms? If there is to be any kind of costume then why and who is to design it? Who is to make the necessary costumes or robes, head-dresses, masks etc? And who is to pay for this? If there is no money, is there some other way? Can the costumes be improvized, and if so, how?

6. *Properties*: What objects are required – candles, candlesticks, bread, wine, water, bowls, flowers, flags, effigies, banners? Again, who is to provide or make them?

7. *Design*: Who is to control the overall design and colour scheme, and co-ordinate all the materials used?

8. *Choreography*: Movements used in a ritual may be circular, with the groups facing inwards or outwards; the circles may be standing still or in motion. The circles may spiral, loop the circle, form figures of eight, concentric circles or double circles, with individuals spinning and turning. The movements may be linear or angular in formation, with avenues of people, perhaps with their arms lifted forming an arch; or in opposing lines, advancing towards one another, criss-crossing, or forming diagonals, squares, stars; moving slowly, or racing forward, skipping, hopping, jumping, leaping. The rich heritage of dances created by the Shakers in America for their meetings for worship demonstrates many of these possibilities, together with words spoken or sung, interspersed with shouts, cries and glossalia, while the whole mood and tempo of the meeting would swing from the Apollonian to the Dionysiac. Anna Halprin, in her *Circle the Earth*, a ritual which she leads all

over the world, uses many of these patterns. The use of the circle as a central motif is found repeatedly in sacred rituals, as also in children's games, providing a centre of security and reassurance, and reaching its finest expression in the Sufi tradition of whirling dervish dances which achieve a controlled and serene spinning 'at the still point of the turning world'. All who have done circle dances testify not only to the sense of equality but also to a strong sense of psychic power focusing the energies of those present.

In evolving a new ritual there has to be an overall movement structure and it has to be rehearsed. Even within Christian churches, as Bill Jardine Grisbrooke wrote in *Liturgical Reform and Liturgical Renewal*, 'the performance of the greatest drama of all in the average church is of a standard which would disgrace the worst of amateur theatrical companies. Most clergy have no idea of the correct use of the body, of how to carry themselves, of how to walk and stand and sit, of how to perform gestures and so on.' Both the celebrants (performers) and observers (worshippers) need to know what they are meant to do at any particular moment and where they are meant to be. If there are to be many hundreds of people taking part, as in a major pilgrimage or a public event, a series of guides (leaders) will have to be trained in order to lead sections of the gathering. It is essential that everything be rehearsed and not left, haphazardly, to chance. If the ritual calls for a procession then the route has to be worked out in detail as well as what happens along the route. In Poland, in Holy Week, the Celebration of the Sufferings of the Lord, which is attended annually by some 50,000 people, re-enacts the major events of Holy Week, culminating in the crucifixion, not on a stage, but before a series of twenty-four chapels spread out over a distance of 6 miles. The events are not compressed into a few hours but continue for a week, with people standing and journeying in mud and rain. It is perhaps not surprising that in recent years those with an interest in the avant-garde in theatre have been especially attracted to these celebrations all over Poland for, as Marjorie S. Young says in her introduction to *Journeys to Glory*, 'here they find a drama in which there is virtually no barrier between actor and spectator, an experience which truly engages the audience'. The outpouring of art from Poland, and the richness of its theatre, with such key figures as Tadeusz Kantor, Josef Szajna, Jerzy Grotowski and many more, stems from a histrionic genius in the national character; a deeply emotional people, they have retained a close access to their emotions as well as to a rich and varied expression of them. It is not surprising that Karol Wojtyla, now Pope John Paul II, when he was Bishop of Krakow, improvized many rituals, gatherings and pilgrimages up into the mountains, nor that in his early years he wanted to be an actor, and wrote plays.

Anything planned for a public space will call for liaison with the police and local authority, and those along the route will have to be warned in advance. In New York there are many public processions throughout the year and for these there is a highly sophisticated procedure to be followed. If the ritual is to take place in the country, perhaps a procession and a celebration of the eucharist in the open air, then it is essential to check with local farmers beforehand. A farmer or landowner has the right to refuse permission for an event on their land, unless it is on an established right of way, and even then it is important to notify everyone concerned.

Whatever movement, gesture or dance is to be used needs planning and rehearsing, although certain sections may be left open for the spontaneous response of the moment. As in the theatre, actors must not be so drilled that they lose their spontaneity. Once actors have mastered a style for a particular production they then have to 'breathe' their performances, 'inhabit' them, so that at every performance, while the overall structure and detail remain the same, fresh emphases, new details, are discovered with every performance. There are some clergy who would maintain that everything must be done strictly to form, without any variation whatsoever.

I used to give simple exercises to an order of Benedictine monks, whose Abbot was anxious that I improve their level and quality of speaking, so that they need not be dependent upon the use of the microphone in the Abbey church. One exercise consisted of inviting the individual to go into the church, ascend the pulpit and imagine he was about to preach to a congregation, speaking the words of introduction, 'In the name of the Father and of the Son and of the Holy Ghost.' He had then to imagine that he was about to preach to a small huddle of people, some six or seven, on an icy cold winter's morning; or to the Sunday high mass when the church would be packed with the entire school which was attached to the Abbey, and to imagine all that highly charged male energy of teenagers. One particular monk, a newly ordained priest, refused to do the exercise, saying 'I would always say mass in the same way!'

Lastly, but most obviously, who is to create, or choreograph, the movement? Will it be one person, or will it, over a period of weeks or months, emerge and evolve from within the group?

9. *Text*: Is there to be a text, either of words or sounds? Are existing texts to be used and if so has permission been obtained from publishers and authors? Or is a new text to be created for the occasion and if so who is to create it? Is it to be the responsibility of one person or, again, is it to evolve from within the group? If sounds are to be used, are these to be made live by those taking part, or mechanically with the use of tape recorders and amplification? Is a composer to be employed and if so at what point is she or he to be brought in? If vocal sounds are to be used (chanting, etc.) how are these to be arrived at, what exercises used in advance? Is the sound to be localized, such as a choir situated in another room or on a balcony (as in Orthodox churches), at a distance or even a long way off. Are the observers (worshippers) to take any part in the text, speaking, singing or chanting? If so, when and how? Should they be given a short rehearsal before the ritual commences or not?

10. *Lighting*: How will the event be illuminated? By natural light, by candle or night lights; by flares, electricity, or moonlight? Is light to be used manually — for example, are people to carry candles? If so, what are the existing fire and safety regulations? And how do you prevent candle grease getting over

everything, especially when children are taking part? Is use to be made of sparklers or fireworks? The use of electric lighting, spotlights and dimmers, can help to create a greater sense of atmosphere, enhancing the beauty and structure of a building as well as the occasion. Part of the appeal of candlelit carol services is the sense of intimacy and domesticity created. Harsh lights, and neon strip lighting most especially, should be avoided in all places of worship.

11. *Sequel*: What is to happen when the ritual comes to a close? If those taking part have been lifted out of themselves, how can we bring them gently back to earth? Is there to be a space for silence, for meditation, for sharing in some way? (But *not* a discussion, which merely reduces the experience to a cerebral debate. Any discussion should come at a later date when everyone has had time to absorb the experience.) Depending upon the numbers involved, a shared meal is the ideal way of helping people to touch down again. I recall the healing impact of such a meal in a small chapel in North Wales where I had gone to represent a close friend who was in Japan, and whose brother, a local farmer, had died. The chapel was packed with uncles, aunts, cousins, all the inhabitants of that small farming community in the hills and mountains. After the funeral there was a tea in the room at the back of the chapel. Here trestle tables had been set end to end, covered with linen cloths and loaded with plates of sandwiches, home-made cakes and large enamel pots of tea. Everyone sat down at this long table. On the walls were faded sepia photographs of former chapel elders and preachers and outings. Aunts, uncles, cousins, neighbours, friends, all sat down to tea. Soon everyone was changing places, moving around, exchanging anecdotes and memories of the young farmer who had died; people embraced and laughed and wept, so that the pain of the occasion was gently dissipated.

Change and experiment in ritual, especially sacred, cannot be imposed from the top, by committees. True change has to start at the grassroots, with small groups. Of course there is a danger that experimentation can lead to self-indulgence (bad theatre!), and

become a series of ego trips and ego strips. And the clergy themselves are not always the best people to initiate change in religious
rituals. Sometimes it can be advantageous to bring in an outsider,
who is both sensitive to the needs of a group and yet sufficiently
detached from it to see what is needed. Thus Anna Halprin of the
Tamalpa Institute in California described to me how a local rabbi
had invited her and her colleagues to revitalize the Friday night
meeting service. *Collectively*, (and I deliberately emphasize the
word) they evolved a new ritual involving the cantor, the rabbi
and her dancers. As a result the synagogue introduced other
changes into the service which involved the participation of the
whole congregation, the women as well as the men. This is not an
isolated example. Many Jewish women, disturbed by the exclusion
of women, have been coming together to rewrite and restructure
certain Jewish ceremonies such as the Haggadah. Judith Plaskow, in
an essay entitled *Bringing a Daughter into the Covenant*, describes
how traditionally boys have been welcomed into the Jewish community with far more pomp and ceremony than have girls. At
eight days they are initiated into the covenant of Abraham in the
dramatic ceremony of *brit milah* (covenant of circumcision). Girls,
on the other hand, are named in the synagogue in the course of a
regular Sabbath service. The father is called to the Torah, generally in
the absence of mother and child, and little marks the event as a
unique and joyous occasion. 'In the past few years,' writes Judith
Plaskow, 'many Jewish parents, myself included, have tried to
rectify this inequality in life cycles by creating distinctive ceremonies for the birth of a daughter, paralleling the *brit milah*.' She
concludes her introduction to the ceremony which she wrote with
these words; 'I hope there will come a time when the exclusion of
women, and therefore insistence on their inclusion, will be an
anachronism. Since for me, full participation of women in the
Jewish community is indissolubly connected with our willingness
to speak of God as male and female, I use female God language
in the ritual. It, like the ceremony as a whole, is deliberately
compensatory.'

Within the Christian churches when does one ever hear of a
whole congregation coming together weeks, or even months, in
advance, to prepare for a particular feast? I think often of the Feast

of Candlemas which marks the occasion when Mary and Joseph brought the baby to the temple to be blessed. This is usually marked by an ambulatory procession around the church, carrying candles (the symbol of the new light which has come into the world with the birth of the Christ), and singing a hymn. Occasionally a baby may be carried in the procession. But there is so much more to the story which would result in something more profound and creative if a group of people were to meet regularly to explore and create their own ritual for this occasion. We read how the couple, and there is no reason why we should not think of them as a young couple, have made the long and arduous journey to the temple in Jerusalem, where they meet two elderly people, Simeon and Anna: the latter, we read, is 'a widow who is eighty-four years of age'. It is unusual in the Gospels to have so specific a detail. And on this particular day we are told that Anna, who never left the Temple, serving God night and day with prayer and fasting, 'came by just at that moment', just as we read of Simeon that 'prompted by the Spirit he came to the Temple'. Already in this story we see how the principle of synchronicity is at work – each might so easily have missed their moment, especially among the thousands of pilgrims arriving daily in the Temple. Simeon forsees that Mary will have to endure much suffering: 'A sword will pierce your heart also so that the secret thoughts of many may be laid bare.' Now any group of actors faced with this story would search first for the main themes and then for the story's subtext, its hidden meanings, examining it from the point of view of each of the characters in turn: Joseph, Mary, the baby, Simeon, Anna, passing rabbis and fellow pilgrims.

One of the central themes is the encounter between the generations, between the very young and the very old. The story invites such questions as: Why do so many of us feel threatened by the elderly and not want to get involved? Why are we so often impatient with the aged, or talk to them as though they were mentally deficient? Is it a fear of our own ageing, that we cannot bear the thought that one day we shall be like that? What is the process of ageing? What role do the aged have in society today, if any? What is the role of the family today? Does the archetype of the Holy Family have anything to say today? In addition, the story has much to say to us about woman in her threefold capacity: as maiden, as mother, and as hag (the wise old woman). As Carol P. Christ points out in her paper, *Why Women Need the Goddess*, 'Western culture gives little dignity to the postmenopausal or ageing woman. It is no secret that our culture is based on a denial of ageing and death, and that women suffer more severely from this denial than men. Women are placed on a pedestal and considered powerful when they are young and beautiful, but they are said to lose this power as they age.' As a woman friend remarked recently to me, 'I have now reached the age in which I have become invisible as a woman so far as men are concerned.'

Quite clearly, any group of women, or women and men and young people, meeting regularly to share their collective experiences, would begin to create a ritual for Candlemas that would be so much more meaningful than the usual pious ambulatory procession. It is when people are entrusted with creating their own rituals, or evolving variants from existing rituals, that such rituals become like lanterns, lit from within. As Tom Driver has written: 'A ritual grows as we grow. What we learn by doing ritual is not only the ritual and how it has been performed before. We discover how to do it next time.'

Christmas is a festival which resonates with images of light shining through the surrounding darkness, evoking in the western hemisphere archaic memories of the dying sun (god) and the celebration of the winter solstice with prayers that the sun (god) might revive and light return to the darkening world. Writing to me recently about the widespread fascination with the occult, a priest observed that it obviously 'provides for a religious need which the Church is not satisfying, and also it expresses *a desire to participate in the rite and not merely sit as passive spectators.*' Those engaged in white witchcraft, or the revival of the Wicca religious practices and beliefs are, he argues, 'surely creative in finding and expressing their own symbols which open them to the divine and to the bodily sharing in the great movement of the seasons and the elements.'

Why has the Church lost this? Why are we content to let so much creativity evade us? Why the fear of allowing the remoulding and new minting of given things, or of letting them rise to new life and expression from within ourselves? Is it, in fact, the clerical desire to control? The panic that 'if once we let *this* happen, then *next* . . .'? The task which faces all religious institutions is how to open up to change. The challenge remains, as Dom Sebastian Moore, OSB, put it in 1970: 'As *man* opens up, bewilderingly, to his depths, and knows newly that they are his, so must the *church* open up and accept a freer, less systematic, and more variegated presence of spiritual power in its members.' To that I would add the following variation 'As *woman* opens up, bewilderingly, to her depths, and knows newly that they are hers, so must the *church* open up and accept a freer, less systematic, and more variegated presence of spiritual power in its members.' While many women continue to work within their own religious traditions and to effect change from within, many more have abandoned the churches and synagogues, and set up their own spirituality groups, shaking off the centuries old domination of men.

Men are moved by dreams, by the images that haunt them, by the ideal pictures that sway their minds — the words they utter, the acts they perform are determined by their imagination. In the same way, the ideal forms of minerals, plants, animals shape the single members of the species. Every rose seed contains the dream, the incorporeal image of a full-blown rose, and this dream can be sensed at work slowly unfolding the rose-buds or causing the green leaves to sprout gently on the stem.

The day one starts sensing the invisible dreams urging rocks, seeds, bodies and minds all around us along their predestined courses the first step towards wisdom has been taken. To achieve this *we should meditate on the images we carry within us; we should become aware of how they are constantly impelling us to think certain thoughts or to make certain gestures.*

Elemire Zolla

IX

Dickson's Journal

Dickson Musslewhite was a student at Colorado College, Colorado Springs, where I was invited to teach a course on ritual. He was unusual in that he was the only student who volunteered for the course who did not have a performing arts background, but was a student of literature and philosophy. The difficulties that he experienced, and the frankness with which he recounts them, and the discoveries that he made, make his account the most telling of all I have read. I remain indebted to the challenge and the reward of his contribution.

Tuesday, 9 April 1985

I came into the class today with a renewed scepticism. I'm not sure where the feeling comes from but I know it was here. I had no choice but to know. For the first half of the class I sat to one side while we performed the exercises. While James explained the exercises, their purpose, their method, I sat in the back and entertained nasty thoughts. What is this bullshit anyway? Am I at a summer camp or a college? These mystical exercises are complete crap. I don't buy it. At $1000 down the drain, I could have gotten in an English class, philosophy, biology, physics, hell, an economic class – anything but this bullshit, this fucking bullshit that is really pissing me off. Ah . . . but how one's mind changes. That was before the break. I was pissed, pissed that I didn't fit into the class and pissed that I didn't have the sense to check out.

98

We had an exercise using a rope. Hanging on to the rope in groups of six we were told to close our eyes and then recreate birth, maturation, then the celebration of the mature state, and death; and, if we wished, rebirth. Going into the exercise I held the same distaste that had gripped me before the break. However, when I emerged from the exercise I felt fresh, calm; I understood the class. I came to understand myself, only a small part of myself, but I still learned something. Throughout the exercise images flashed through my head. In the other exercises there were no images, just aggressive, dissatisfied thoughts. I don't know what brought on the leap from dissatisfied thoughts to images – the answer to that question might bring on some answers to the other bigger questions. I do know that the leap was big. The images were and are important.

The particular image that struck me came in the process of maturation. On the outside I was physically holding on to the rope and struggling to stand; I was doing a feeble job of acting out the difficulty of standing, of maturing. On the inside it was different; in my imagination I clearly thought out and answered the difficulty of standing.

There was a shore. I stood on the shore with the cooling sand pressed against my feet and between my toes, as I sadly watched the tide slip away. The tide was leaving and I was left alone. A rush of emptiness soared into my mind, my body, my whole being, just as it had when I experienced the death of a very important relationship. The relationship died in my senior year in high school. It had been two years since this death but, subconsciously, and sometimes consciously, this death still held my mind. The girl was very special to me and remained very special until my image of her received a gashing axe wound. That was two years ago, but I hadn't overcome the feeling of emptiness. I shivered as the tide ran out and the sand cooled down.

What happened next in images was very important. I immediately flipped from the dusk scene to a similar scene at dawn. Now, however, the tide floated to my feet. The warm ocean foam filled the cracks in my toes and warmed the sand below. That was it! For two years I had watched the tide flow away. Finally I saw it return. Sure, I often intellectualized the motion of starting over, of finding new love. But now, through the images, I truly understand it. The intellectualization built an empty well. In it I found no real understanding, just a detached comprehension. So hope has returned. Why, I don't know. I don't know why that one specific exercise provided a major breakthrough in understanding this class and understanding my life. Granted the images don't stay by themselves. They need the music of interpretation. But intellectualizing and only intellectualizing never sings. At best it runs.

Tomorrow night might bring a change of opinions. I might enter the class and grumble and curse my way through the morning. But, for now, I know I made the right decision by staying in the class. I know I've learned something that a thousand biology courses would never have shown me, that economics could never teach me. Today I learned hope. With hope I have learned to hunger.

Wednesday, 10 April

Well, I didn't go into class today in a pissed off mood. I went happy and whistling. The first hour or so consisted of the breathing and humming exercises that we have been doing for three days. After those we moved into new, less physical exercises.

Sitting in a circle with our eyes closed, we had to pass images around, from left to right. The person to my left might say 'an ocean', for instance, and I would respond with a detailed description of the first image that popped into my mind. At first the exercise wasn't particularly exciting since the descriptions weren't detailed and the exercise just became word association. However, James corrected our methods and then the purpose of the exercise became apparent. With more detail came a fuller meaning. I stumbled into one particularly nasty image that might be revealing.

The person on my left described a man on a beach, and a circle of people dancing around a fire. The student who was describing this found the image comforting and sought companionship in the circle. However I found it horrifying. Seen from the outside, looking at the backs of the heads of the people, the circle appeared benign. But as I moved into the circle the truth of the circle was revealed. It opened like a jaw, a vicious hungry jaw, in which were twenty or so gleaming faces. The firelight danced on the faces. It danced with lustful flickerings on the distorted faces of these cannibals, yes, cannibals. It was an image that grew in my mind from William Golding's novel, *Lord of the Flies*. Seeing the horror inside the circle spurred in me a great desire to leave. All I could think was, 'Dickson, get the fuck out of here!' Unfortunately it was too late. Had I kept my distance from the circle I would have been fine. I was a victim of my own curiosity. Or maybe, and probably, I was a victim of my inability to stand aloof. I tried to leave the circle but couldn't. Quickly, aggressively, the cannibals took hold of me. I fought desperately but it was no use. Their strength was too great.

They strapped me to a crucifix which they stood in the fire. It was a raging fire around which they danced merrily as I burned. Here the image ended as the exercise ended. I didn't explain the crucifixion to the other students. I didn't want to. While others described their images I *lived* this crucifixion. So what does the image mean? I think my mind developed in imagery the concept of sacrifice. It wasn't a good concept of sacrifice. And it was a sacrifice that developed from the inability to stand alone. But the crucifixion contradicts that, for Christ stood alone, as alone as a human being could possibly stand. Perhaps I have no choice but to stand alone, or so my mind thinks. My desire to belong will betray me and leave me more alone than ever. It is one thing to be alone and unseen. And it is completely different to be alone and the spectacle. Nothing highlights loneliness more than loneliness observed.

All this talk of loneliness takes me away from the specific image to the broader subject of the class. In two days I have had two images, very strong images, that depicted my loneliness. The effect of ritual helps men, in general, circumvent this loneliness. That much I know through the experience of humming in the class.

However, James seems to push us to a better sense of self-identity. He constantly pushes us to work with imagery that emphasizes individuality. So how does his desire to make us individuals coincide with the performance of rituals? The ritual, the chanting and humming, whitewash our individuality. The rituals make a collective unit where individuals are non-existing. Is this fact a contradiction between the nature of the class and the nature of James's personality? Or have I misinterpreted? These questions hopefully will be answered soon. If I emerge from the class without an answer to one of the questions, if not all of them, then I will have wasted my time.

Thursday, 11 April

At 9.00 this morning I was puking my guts out. While birds chirped outside in the cool mountain air, I was throwing up. While students gleefully headed towards class, refreshed with a full night's sleep, I was puking. I was puking and James was lecturing. He didn't find an early morning fraternity party a proper excuse for absence. I think that only death and sickness are proper excuses. What James did not know was that I was so sick I was wishing I was dead.

Actually there is no excuse for this morning's absence, but it might be worthwhile to explore the early morning events anyway. What I experienced this morning involved a ritual developed by the Colorado College chapter of Beta Theta Phi. The ritual consecrates the friendship between the pledge fathers and pledge sons. A pledge father is an active Beta, someone who is already a member of the fraternity, who is supposed to take a pledge son, someone who wishes to be a fraternity member, under his wing and show him the ropes. I am a pledge father. My pledge son, like the other pledge sons, decided to show his appreciation for my commitment to him by waking me up on this fine sunny mountain morning and getting me drunk. Unfortunately he showed his appreciation much too well and I found myself to be not only drunk but also sick.

The 'Wake-up', as it's called, has been a part of Beta life since the early 1950s. It has consecrated friendship of pledge father and pledge son for nearly thirty years. Not only does 'Wake-up' as a ritual confirm a special step in the life of fraternity members but it does so in a symbolic manner. In general, the members of Beta hold drinking and drugs up as sacred objects. The purpose of the fraternity is to help its members enjoy themselves. The fraternity espouses a hedonistic philosophy, and alcohol and drugs are the sacraments of the rituals, all of the rituals, that affirm our belief in this philosophy. Therefore 'Wake-up' was not only a confirmation of specific friendship but it was also an affirmation of the whole fraternity's philosophy.

Friday, 12 April

Ken Kesey said, 'You're either on the bus or you're off the bus.' He said it to a member of the Merry Pranksters, a group of youths who were experimenting with LSD in the 1960s and of which he was in charge. The member had been violating the sense of unity of the group that was pushing itself out, into 'edge city'. He just wasn't on the bus.

Right now I feel 'off the bus'. The bus is this course. Instead of LSD the class uses certain near-eastern and drama exercises to explore and push the students to 'edge city'. Right now, I don't feel involved with this exploration. Earlier in the week I explored some through a single image. The following day I had another image. Since those two days I've had no images and have felt nothing but resentment – resentment at being in the class, but not really being there. Am I wasting my time?

Talking to other members of the group doesn't help me much either. Whenever I ask them what they think about the class, they always answer me with unquestioning excitement, 'Oh, I really like it!'

'Well, what *do* you like about it?'

'Oh, James is just the greatest!'

'. . . Hmm, I see.'

Fuck! Is that all? Yes, I know that James is great. I like James a lot. But that doesn't mean that his *class* is great. Why is it great for them and not for me? Why are they so sure of themselves and the class and I am struggling? Maybe they're just different. No, that's definitely a cop out. I feel that there is something crucial, incredibly beneficial about this class, but I don't *know* that. Right now I'm wavering. I've got one foot on the first stair of the 'bus' and one foot on the pavement. Today James read a letter, or journal entry, of a student who was faced with the same predicament. He was in a class of James's. He found everyone involved in the class but himself. Determined to learn, he decided to throw himself into the class with reckless abandon. He had nothing to lose and everything to gain.

Today I will make that same vow – no more drunken mornings, no more self-pity. I am now dedicated to the class. If I fail, I will have lost no more than if I didn't try.

Monday, 15 April

Class wasn't particularly exciting today. The exercises have already grown wearisome and I find myself slipping in enthusiasm. My hands can clutch the rock no longer. That is how I felt during the actual class today, just repetitious. We continue to perform the same exercise and rightly so. Theoretically, understanding would occur through familiarization with one exercise. The person who is familiar with one exercise should be able to really express themselves fully; as opposed to a person who knows several exercises but is not really familiar with them. Seen through one window, the view is much clearer than when it is seen fragmentarily through several windows.

I know this intellectually but not spiritually. Intellectually I tell myself to work with the frontier exercise, to make use of it. Spiritually I tell myself that the exercise is uninteresting, unstimulating, it offers no avenues on which my imagination may travel. So, today, the frontier exercise grew wearisome. Intellectually I am making great strides with the work. As James said, the Joseph Campbell book *The Hero with a Thousand Faces* is really interesting. Campbell brings together many ideas that I have been playing with over the past years. His formalization of the heroic life brings the great scattering of my literary background into one focused image. Last night, after having read the Campbell, I thought of all the books that I could remember. I really couldn't remember that many but the ones I could remember fit the Campbell. That is those books and tales of great heroic ventures fit nicely into the separation-initiation-return formula. From Shane to Christ — Campbell is right.

One interesting idea that might not be so interesting, that in fact may be obvious, invokes Plato. While Campbell described the heroic mono-myth, I kept thinking of the Analogy of the Cave. Plato describes a cave where the occupants are bound. They are bound so that they can only look forward towards the end of the cave, where shadowy images flicker. The images are produced by figures moving before a fire. From this world of images, Plato feels the hero must emerge. He must separate himself from the shadowy life and move to a higher world. For Campbell this is separation. [In Jungian terms, it is only by confronting our shadow side that we can then integrate it into our consciousness. JRE]

What Plato next describes is a journey along a path that emerges from the cave and up into the real world. The journey takes place under the intense rays of sunlight that enter through the exit. The sunlight, symbolizing truth, is painful for the hero, whose eyes are accustomed only to the shadowy light of the images. Once he has reached the exit, the hero discovers a world of unbelievable ecstasy that tempts him. But, as Plato says, the hero must return to the cave if he is to do any good. Once past the initiation stage, the journey, he must venture to the world of shadows in order to free people from a life of shadows. That is the return. That, according to Joseph Campbell, is the crucial step in a hero's journey.

Well, I think I am enjoying the class intellectually, but spiritually it just isn't clicking. Spiritually I peaked with the image exercise last week. I hope there is another peak on the other side of this valley.

Tuesday 16 April

Today went better than expected. Although I had ample opportunity to increase my disinterest in the exercises, as we repeated the frontier exercise twice today, I actually found myself more interested. I think that there is, after all, another peak on the other side of this valley. The first frontier exercise wasn't particularly exciting for me. The motions felt contrived and the images were forced. Nothing really flowed.

However, the second time actually held understanding, through the images of course. I think that the difference in the efficacy of the exercise stemmed from the difference in the amount of effort that I put into each of them. In the frontier exercise on Monday and the first one today I didn't concentrate from the beginning, hoping that the exercise would develop as I drew nearer to the frontier. That didn't happen.

In the second frontier exercise today I changed my strategy. Concentrating from the beginning, I developed a theme, a central idea, before I even moved. In my mind I pictured a girl, a Colorado College student, whom I have observed from a distance but have actually never talked to. She is quite beautiful and her beauty often captivates my imagination. I pictured this girl, European in appearance, with blonde hair; I pictured her as I know her – from a distance. As I moved, crawling first on my belly, then on my hands and knees and, finally, walking upright, so I drew nearer to her. My images changed from a distant picture of her alone to close-ups of her and me together. The images luckily weren't limited to sexual pictures. I often found myself moving in an active daydream of a long life with this girl, of love, of true love, and the full range of activities that love consists of. I learned of the benefits and the commitments needed. I learned of the need and the desires of both her and me. The images of the two of us were closest and clearest after I first stood up, about halfway through the exercise. Then they grew distant and dull. In the end I found myself lying on the frontier. I'm not sure exactly what inspired me to lie down on the frontier but in retrospect the action makes complete sense.

The frontier was the passage from life into death. The journey began, as it should, from my present state of mind. The journey focused on a love affair that lasted the rest of my life. It was a love that enabled me to beat the loneliness of death. With love I lost the existential hunger that constantly spears me at this stage in my life. I found a fuller sense of life that filled in the black hole of expectation of death that plagues the hungry human. I don't think that I could have lived this love had it not been for the exercise. I merely would have remained contented with the sexual fantasies of my daydream. I don't know if the feeling and understanding spanned by the exercise will remain, or if it will subside, as actual love subsides, but I know that today I experienced love and can enjoy it, at least for a day.

Wednesday, 17 April

After seeing some slides we did a candle exercise. First we sat in a circle with a lit candle in the middle, and described the images that the candle encourages. That was fun because I kept pretending that we were sitting round a campfire. I always enjoy that. After watching the single candle, we each lit individual candles. James went through a description of the candle as a symbol of ideas and the human life and the influence that each can have on one another, other humans, other candles. From this each of us developed our own symbols ... I think I enjoyed today's workshop because I enjoy firelight, and the way it makes me feel inside. The ideas and the images surrounding this light.

Friday, 19 April

Fun. Fun. Fun. Loveable Friday was exceptionally loveable today. During class we took on a new exercise, remembering and acting out children's games. I can't say that the exercise produced many images or much understanding but it was fun as hell. I suppose one thing to remember from today is how much fun remembering can be when it is taken in proper proportions. After this we broke into groups in an attempt to develop our own rituals. The exercise failed miserably and shed light on our ineptitude concerning the concept of ritual. We really did not know what a ritual is. And James had to define a ritual. It was a twelve-line definition that certainly left me feeling stupid. How could I be so naïve and yet so unconcerned about my naïvety? Something to think about.

A ritual is a journey.

A true ritual should lead the spirit into an inner realm.

The most sacred of all rituals will lead to an encounter with the
     Divine.
A true ritual should open up a space into which the Spirit may
     enter.
At the centre and heart of true ritual is silence ... deep, con-
     tented, grave, awesome and joyous.
The true ritual takes ordinary things; bread, wine, cloth, table,
     candles, fire, and enables us to perceive the extra-ordinariness
     beyond ...
We have to be focused, disciplined, centred, made aware.

Sometimes I think that 50 per cent of my education is a lie. Yup,
about one half of the time. I stay in school for grades and parental
appeasement. What a chicken shit. That certainly is a lie and the
one I'm lying to is myself. Learning should spring from curiosity. If
I don't want to learn something, then I'm obviously not curious
... It's not just the school or the fact that I'm lonely angers me. I
think it has something to do with life in general. Sitting around, I
see that I'm not the only one who's unhappy. Hell, most of this
campus is unhappy. And those that aren't unhappy are either too
stupid or don't give a shit. But maybe that's the answer. Actually I
think I've tried that before, and look where I am. Oh well, this has
got to end before my anger surfaces again: *Vanitas vanitatis*.

Saturday, 27 April

I'm glad that we had to keep a journal. It was definitely a pain in
the arse at times, but, in the end, it was worth it. The pages of a
journal, the blank pages, are finer then any mirror. In a mirror the
images come very easily, there is no struggle. In a real mirror the
image is but a physical image. On the page it is the struggle that
makes it true. And the truth is a spiritual truth. Thanks, James.
Dickson.

                    *   *   *

At one stage everyone was invited to write a prayer 'to a known or
an unknown God'. Here is Dickson's:

With the unsecuring sea stretching
before me,
To mystery
I make my pledge.
To search
To swim
To dive as deep as I can.

With the unsecuring sea stretching
before me,
To mystery
I give my thanks.
For you I am thankful
With you I am,
Without you I am not.

Ritual is indeed a voyage into the unknown. To quote Emily Dickinson once again:

Exultation is the going
Of the soul to sea:
Past the houses, past the headland,
Into deep Eternity!

Those who, like Dickson, have the courage to make a commitment, who are prepared to search, to dive as deep as they can, will always find the sunken treasure hidden deep within themselves. For those who will confront the mystery and accept their destiny, there will always be profound gratitude, for, with Walt Whitman, they may truly say: 'Now in a moment I know what I am for and a thousand songs spring to life within my breast!' The loneliness which Dickson learned to confront is to be found among thousands of students on the campuses of America, although College authorities often conveniently choose to deny this. I know because I have listened to so many of these students. Yet, in confronting his existential loneliness Dickson was to learn, as did Emily Dickinson, that:

. . . Loneliness — [is]
The Maker of the soul
Its caverns and its corridors
Illuminate or seal.

X

The Exercises

'What is this bull-shit anyway?'
Dickson Musslewhite

INTRODUCTION

New exercises are constantly evolving but I include here only those which have been tested and refined over many years in the fire of workshops. In each of the exercises the individual is confronted with an image to which she or he is invited to give a total response: physical, emotional, imaginative. Vocal sound may be used but no dialogue or words. The exercises must always be prefaced by some form of centring down, using Shinto or other breathing exercises followed by vocal exercises. These are described in the first section. Without such centring down the response to the exercises is likely to be merely cerebral or superficial. The more we invest ourselves in the exercises the more we will get out of them. Unlike psycho-drama which operates primarily on a level of acting out certain life situations, these exercises are more like conscious dreaming, revealing some aspect of the interior landscape of each person. Here is how one young woman described the experience of doing the hand exercise.

FROM ANITA'S JOURNAL

I have discovered that the hand exercise is very indicative of my mood. For example, today I found myself reaching out in search of contact, but no contact was made. My hands searched straight ahead, then to right and left and behind me, finding nothing. They moved along the ground, in mid-air, and high above my head, still finding nothing. At one point they grasped and held each other as if to compensate for the futile search, but the comfort they sought was not there. Although I did not know it while the exercise was in progress, when James gave us a few minutes to think about what had transpired, it occurred to me that this is how I have been thinking this past week. I was hoping that a friendship I had with someone would develop into something more personal, but this week my friend tells me that he met a very nice girl whom he has been dating regularly, and that he won't have much time to talk to me any more. Today I am still hurting a bit.

Thus does a simple exercise bring to the surface unacknowledged (and sometimes unconscious) conflicts or yearnings, and giving expression to them in this way enables the individual to contemplate what is happening and to absorb it into their conscious awareness.

I always stress that the effects of this work may be therapeutic but it is not intended as therapy as such, but should be regarded as performance. All of us are, in fact, performers; we all play many roles in our daily lives, but the more we are aware of this the better performers we can become, and not be trapped in our roles. To this end, as Stanislavsky observed of the professional actor, although 99 per cent of the performer may be identifying with what is happening, allowing feelings and emotions to flow through him or her, there is always 1 per cent that is controlling and shaping what is happening; if there were not, an individual might freak out, become possessed. It is this aspect of control which makes the choices in an exercise, which shapes what is unfolding, with the result that there is never any danger that we may physically hurt ourselves or another person. If I feel anger when I am doing one of the exercises then I have to choose how to express it through a movement, a sound or rhythm, shaping the feeling. As in Zen we allow ourselves to be acted upon by something deep in our natures; we are an instrument which is played upon willingly. We allow the dream to dream us. 'It is as though the emotions are pouring out of the hands', as one person expressed it. It is only when the exercise is completed that we can meditate upon and, at a later stage, analyse what has transpired. In his autobiography Carl Jung refers to certain tribes in Africa who 'act first and do not know what they are doing. Only long afterwards do they reflect on what they have done.'

We are not asked to act out a story or to write a script in advance; if we do, the results will always be still-born. But if, out of our stillness and concentration we respond to the most power-ful image that arises within us, and if we allow ourselves to go with it, then we shall be led to a conclusion that we could not have foreseen, imagined or even planned. Rather, we shall be overtaken and surprised by images hidden in our unconscious. If a strong movement or gesture occurs we must not be afraid to repeat it rhythmically, over and over, until of its own volition it will lead us into the next movement or gesture and so on. Similarly we must not be afraid of stillness, so long as it does not become a state of passivity. It was said of the great American modern dancer Martha Graham that she could just stand on stage absolutely still and yet the effect was like watching the Niagara Falls. Stillness, like a rest in music, is important. But once an image has appeared then we must go with it and not restlessly keep trying to change it. If, for example, my first image is of a bird (perhaps trapped and wanting to escape, or hovering above a landscape, or hatching its cluster of eggs), I must learn to keep my attention on this image and not allow the 'bird' to escape until it has explained to me what message it brings me from the unconscious. Otherwise the monkey mind with its ceaseless chatter will turn the bird into a lion into a ship at sea into a tree and so on, image dissolving into image as in a kaleido-scope. We must not allow the exercise to become a form of mental cinema. Afterwards, as we reflect, we may begin to see that it is some aspect of ourselves which is trapped and wanting to escape, or hovering over a situation pondering where to land, or experienc-ing a need to cherish that which we have created and bring it to birth. The shaping spirit of the imagination, if we trust it, will lead us on this voyage into unknown waters, this journey into our own interior landscape. The creative intelligence, however, provides the reins of control. But it takes time and patience and a number of false starts before one begins to progress.

Each of us is unique and our feelings are peculiar to each one of us. It is our task to find the exact expression of those feelings. As Herbert Read once wrote, 'Art is an instrument for tilling the human psyche that it may continue to yield a harvest of rich beauty.' The common failure, as he remarked, is to allow habitual words and responses 'to flow spontaneously from the memory and *de*-form the feeling rather than *in*-form it.' The whole exercise, he concludes, is one of exquisite perception and instinctive judgement. We have to learn how to sit loosely to the exercise until it takes over for and from us. With practice we shall also learn how to recognize when an exercise has come to a conclusion or when it has simply reached a point of rest and stillness out of which a new phase may begin – if we wait.

If I have stressed the importance of centring down and of concentration it is because so much confusion still exists in association with the word 'improvisation', even in the professional theatre, and all too often is merely self-indulgent, a general emoting. This is why the fine conscious control of the individual is so important; it is this which gives permission for the unconscious images to emerge, and which then selects and chooses, out of a myriad of choices, sensing and encouraging the underlying pattern which is seeking to reveal itself.

'A true game is one that frees the spirit.' The true game, as Locke recognized years ago, is the one that arises from the players themselves.

OPENING AND CLOSING RITUALS: BINDING AND GROUNDING

Introduction

Each workshop should commence with a simple ritual which marks the participants' turning away from their everyday preoccupations and turning in towards the inner space which they are about to explore. Similarly, at the end, and especially because the work takes people deep within themselves, it is essential to have a closing ceremony which serves to ground each person, just as the opening ceremony binds everyone. Participants in this kind of workshop need earthing before they return to their homes and the outside world.

The Naming Ritual

For a group meeting for the first time I use Anna Halprin's *Naming Ritual*. Everyone stands in a circle, and moving clockwise each person speaks his or her first name. The first person speaks their own name, but the second person has to repeat their neighbour's name before speaking their own, until the last person has to speak the name of everybody in the circle before coming to their own name. If there is a large number of people, several circles are formed. It is worth doing this twice, and keeping the whole atmosphere light and relaxed. Now it is followed by . . .

The Name Dance

As above, but as each person speaks their name they have to create a positive gesture or movement. The next person repeats both the movement and the way of speaking their neighbour's name, and then adds their own name and gesture. Clearly it gets more complicated, and hilarious, as it moves round the circle. When it has been done once, it should be repeated but with more confidence. Then a third time. Now, to a drum beat, eliminate the names, and just use the gesture and movements, creating a dance. This can be done to different tempi, speaking or singing the names, or not. If there are several groups doing this in a large workshop, each group should do its name dance for the others. By this means people relax, and get to know each other more swiftly. At the end of the day the whole group comes together and creates its own variation.

The Shinto Opening and Closing Ritual

This I use for an on-going group. Everyone stands in a circle, facing outwards, being aware of the space in which they are standing, the rest of the building, the streets outside, their home, and the world outside. Then, slowly, hands are raised sideways and brought together above the head, palm to palm. Keeping the hands together each person bows to the walls, the building, the outside world, making a deep obeisance. Then all turn inwards, aware of one another, and of the space which they are about to enter. Slowly hands are again raised above the head, palm to palm, and then each person bows deeply to the group and to the space within the circle.

At the end of the workshop, this is reversed, so that everyone is saying farewell to the experience of working together, to the space that has been explored. They then turn to face the outside world which they are about to re-enter, but carrying with them the experience of the workshop.

Simple as this is, it must be done slowly and formally, and in unison.

THE VOCAL WORK

Introduction

We normally think of words in their semantic context, their dictionary meaning; as information rather than as symbols. But as the English poet, Ted Hughes, observed in a radio interview with the playwright Tom Stoppard, 'What you hear in a person's voice is what is going on at the centre of gravity in his consciousness at that moment. When the mind is clear and the experience of that moment is actual and true, then a simple syllable can transmit volumes. A survivor needs only to sigh and it hits you like a hammer. A commentator could chat on for a month and you'd get nothing.'

Hughes argues that there exists in the human race a common tonal consciousness, 'a language belonging below the levels where all differences appear'. Similarly Jung maintained that we all share, at a deeper level, a collective unconscious. That this level can be tapped in sound is demonstrated by John Heilpern in his account of the British theatre director Peter Brook's journey through Africa, especially in the meeting between Brook's actors and a particular tribe called the Peulhs. As soon as the Peulhs began to sing, the American composer, Liz Swados, who was working with the actors, was on her feet, as Heilpern describes.

She knew the Peulh sound went to the heart of everything she's searching for. There is one sustained note, a sound held for so long we weren't even aware of a voice behind it, a sound pure and simple, effortless, it was as if the whole meaning of everything that is so unintelligible and mystifying about life had somehow been shown to us. From where or how, I didn't know. But it was there and it was as if the sound had a life of its own. The sound merged with others, vibrating. It was as if the sounds weren't human. They were beyond art, beyond culture, beyond everything except dreams. 'Music,' wrote Leonardo da Vinci, 'is the shape and form of the invisible.' The Peulhs could capture the invisible, and held the secret.

At once Peter Brook arranged for a private meeting between his actors and the Peulhs. A nomadic tribe, shy of strangers, a mystery even to Africans, with no linking language, how could the actors build a bridge to them in one meeting? There was only one way and it was through music. Brook asked the actors to sing a song. But the Peulhs took no notice, the men just admiring themselves in little mirrors. The actors tried six songs but nothing happened. And then Brook asked for an AH sound [see 'The Vocal Exercises' below], just this one basic sound that was to be extended and developed as far as it could possibly go. It seems an easy thing to do. Yet the group had worked on this one sound for weeks and months. It seemed like an awful moment of truth. The group began to make the sound. The Peulhs were still staring into their mirrors. I watched the actors grow hesitant, uncertain whether to continue. But the sound stretched and grew – and the Peulhs unexpectedly looked up from their mirrors for the first time. The sound took life, vibrating. The Peulhs discarded their mirrors and joined the sound. Oh, it seemed miraculous! It was as if the Peulhs were pulling the sound from them. They pointed to the sky. Just as the unimaginable sound reached its height, or seemed to, no one would venture any further. Somehow it was frightening. The two sides had met and come together in one sound. And yet it was as if they were stunned and frightened by the discovery. Ted Hughes has written of the sounds far beyond human words that open our deepest and innermost ghost to sudden attention ... But now the Peulhs offered an exchange and sang their songs. And they told Brook something very precious. He knew at last that he was on the right road for a universal language. Perhaps we were only beginning to understand. But spirits speak there, in invisible worlds.

The Peulh music showed that a universal language might be as simple as one note repeated many, many times. But the right note must be discovered first. The Peulhs could vary and enrich the sound, changing it in subtle ways, but the strength behind the sound is not made by force. 'Somehow the strength makes itself. With the Peulh everything seemed effortless. Even the sound itself seemed to have a wondrous life of its own ... we were light years behind their "simplicity".'

Both Peter Brook and Liz Swados had talked of the possibility of one note that could become a source, the purest of essence. So much of the group's work had been based on this, that a sound might somehow be found that would encompass and convey an entire feeling. Of course, the performer has first to get at the emotion, to tap those archetypes that lie dormant in the collective unconscious.

'All that has dark sounds,' wrote Garcia Lorca, the Spanish poet and dramatist, 'has *duende*. It is not a matter of ability but of real live form; of blood, of ancient culture; of creative action. To help us seek the *duende* there is neither map nor discipline. All one knows is that it turns blood like powdered glass, that it exhausts, that it rejects all the sweet geometry one has ever learned, that it breaks with all styles.'

There were many who, hearing for the first time the eight-octave voice of Roy Hart, or the sounds created by his company, were disturbed. Such sounds rejected all the sweet geometry they had ever learned. Such sounds, many critics declared, were not human. Yet, as Roy Hart observed, 'Those who can hear without fear know that these sounds which are commanded to come forth are under conscious control.' It was not surprising that composers such as Henze, Stockhausen, and others wanted to compose for Hart's remarkable voice, nor that Peter Maxwell-Davies especially created for him the music-theatre work, *Songs of A Mad King*.

It was in the early 1960s that Peter Brook first visited the Roy Hart Studio in London and was impressed and excited by what he found. In 1966 he returned twice, and also took the innovative Polish theatre director, Jerzy Grotowski, to see and hear their work. The Roy Hart Theatre, which I was privileged to know closely, grew out of the work of Alfred Wolfsohn, who was born in Berlin in 1896 and escaped from Germany in 1938, settling in London where he lived until his death in 1962. Believing that the voice is the audible expression of a man's inner being, he devoted his life to trying to discover why, in most people, the voice is shackled, monotonous, cramped. Through his research he learned that the voice is not the function solely of any anatomical structure but the expression of the whole personality. Working with a great variety of people he proved that the human voice is restricted only by the psychological problems of the individual and that, conversely, the voice is a way through which all aspects of an individual can be developed. His work with singers and actors, as well as with ordinary people, led to an increase in the vocal range, irrespective of sex, from two to eight octaves, even nine.

What Wolfsohn found is that many sounds are produced not by the larynx but by many different parts of the body, from energy centres in the head, chest and stomach, and are resonated throughout the body. These centres were named 'resonators' by Grotowski who, in 1979, publicly acknowledged his debt to the work of Alfred Wolfsohn. To the listener it appears as though the performer is speaking with different parts of the body. Grotowski defined about twenty resonators, and was convinced that others remained to be discovered.

According to legend, Brahman, God himself, was born from the cosmic being's mouth, a notion embedded in the fact that the word *brahman* means 'breath'. I recall Professor Huston Smith telling me about the chanting of Tibetan Buddhist monks at Gyutu Monastery in northern India, whom he had observed at first hand,

and remarking how in the West the question, 'Are you sound?' usually means 'Are you healthy?' whereas in Tibet it would be taken literally as meaning 'Are you not in fact composed of vibrations?'

Believing themselves to be in some sense sound, the lamas are unusually open to influence by what they hear. They feel aligned – or identified – with the sounds they resonate to. And, as Huston Smith has written:

> Since the object of worship is to shift the sacred from peripheral to focal awareness, the vocal capacity to elevate over-tones from subliminal to focal awareness carries symbolic power. For the object of the spiritual quest is precisely this: to experience *life* as replete with over-tones that tell of a 'more' that can be sensed but not seen, sensed but not said, heard but not explicitly. Heard melodies are sweet, but those unheard are sweeter. To consciously, explicitly, hear those 'unheard melodies' is the lamas' unique achievement.

Only two monasteries in all of Tibet have developed this specific art of singing in chords and tones and over-tones, and the training commences at the age of twelve. But the use of the human voice in ritual is still capable of being explored by us in the West, as Alfred Wolfsohn, Roy Hart and his followers, and Jerzy Grotowski, and Peter Brook have demonstrated.

Alfred Wolfsohn believed that there exists in the human voice a common structure which makes it possible that that which is called soprano, contralto, tenor, baritone, or bass, exists in everybody, whether child or adult, male or female. As Maria Guther, one of his pupils, told me, 'He believed that to find the voice, work with it, dredge it out of your depth, pull it out of your guts, would lead to becoming something like a human being.'

In a similar way, Anna Halprin, one of the pioneers in America of ritual-making, has spoken of the links between a person's movement and their psychological growth. 'Whatever emotional, physical and mental barriers we may carry around with us in our personal lives,' she remarked, 'it will be the same barriers that inhibit our full creative expression. It is for this reason that we need to release emotional blocks in order to realize fully our human creative

potential, in terms of being able to develop effectively as performers and creators, as well as to participate with satisfaction in
our lives. I look at emotional blocks as as damaging to artistic
growth as to personal growth.'

Actor, singer, teacher, philosopher, Roy Hart was primarily
concerned with extending the consciousness of man. Like Gurdjieff, he laid great emphasis upon learning how to work, how to
live out fully each moment – a kind of applied Taoism. He was
concerned to pierce the outer shell which we call personality and
to discover, uncover, the essence of the individual. Like Nietzche
he believed that man possesses, as yet largely untapped, enormous
potential. He believed that most people live what he called a one-
octave life, whereas, he maintained, it is possible through work on
the self, through conscious suffering and discipline, to lead an
eight-octave life, the outer expression of which is the eight-octave
voice.

Gurdjieff insisted that a group of people could achieve more
than one person working alone; hence the importance of such
groups as the original Gurdjieff Institute at Fontainebleau, the
Bruderhoff, the Roy Hart Theatre and other similar groups. Asked
whether there is such a thing as destiny, I think that Roy Hart
would have replied with Gurdjieff that only a person with essence
has a destiny: other people are merely subject to the law of accident –
which is the theme of Iris Murdoch's novel, *The Accidental Man*.
Over twenty-five years Roy Hart demonstrated, as had Alfred
Wolfsohn before him, that by releasing psychological tensions and
employing the many resonators in the human body, a fuller and
richer range of emotion and voice can be tapped. At its purest the
Roy Hart Theatre achieved, at certain moments, a transcendental
form of theatre. Technically I think there is little doubt that Roy
Hart was a shaman. Often when attending performances in their
studio I was reminded of these words from Lissner's, *Man, God
and Magic*: 'The shaman's excitement communicates itself to the
circle of spectators and the larger the audience the stronger the
empathy between him and them. They all know each other, being
inter-related and members of the same clan ... the excitement
mounts, leaping like a spark from one man to the next, until all are
near ecstasy, and each is at once performer and spectator, doctor

and patient, hammer and anvil.' And he adds that those assembled around a shaman experience a satisfaction infinitely deeper than we ourselves do after a musical or dramatic performance.

In Shakespeare's *Pericles* Marina heals the King of his madness and melancholia by singing to him. As Otto Jespersen wrote in 1922, 'Men sang out their feelings long before they were able to speak their thoughts.' Similarly, Orpingalik, a famous Eskimo song-maker, observed to Knud Rasmussen, 'Songs are thoughts, sung out with the breath when people are moved by great forces and ordinary speech no longer suffices.' Man's primitive utterances, continues Jespersen, 'were at first like the singing of birds and the roaring of many animals and the crying and crooning of babies, exclamative, not communicative – that is, they came forth from an inner craving of the individual.'

The ancient power of tonal sound, singing without words, to heal and integrate is being discovered afresh in the field of music therapy where many dramatic case histories are now available for examination. One of the most revealing accounts of the power of singing is given by the British anthropologist, Colin Turnbull, in a long essay, *Liminality*, in which he describes his experience of the *molimo*, a ritual belonging to the Mbuti tribe in Zaire, and performed at the time of any crisis but especially on the occasion of a death. Throughout the weeks of the ritual, he was aware that every single action, however serious or however slight, was seen as being 'work'.

That awareness was all that was necessary for my own actions to be in keeping with those of others. And it was here more than ever that total participation paid off, in terms of both what was observed and what was felt. The ideal was not to sleep at all, and in point of fact since the men and male youths sang from dusk to dawn and were strictly forbidden to sleep during this time, there was only about an hour or so of real sleep possible before the day's hunt got under way . . . But if the fatigue was real, so was the stimulation we received from all this work; it was as though the harder we worked the more energy we were given, and the most energy-giving work of all was the nightly singing. And that was when the curing really took place. That was when I felt clean and whole, free of all doubt and worry. It was not that any questions were answered, it was simply that they were removed; at first, at the conscious level, they just became insignificant and inconsequential, then they simply vanished. And that of course was a far more powerful way of getting rid of any problem than the most rational of explanations or answers, for reason can always be made to turn on itself, it is the handmaiden of doubt and suspicion. Here we were safely beyond the reach of mere reason and that rational form of religious experience known as 'belief'. Here we were in the realm of 'faith' and that is why it is so vitally important to distinguish the two, something most anthropologists have neglected sadly, resulting in their often trite and trivial rational, objective 'explanations' of other religious systems. Among the Mbuti there was no room for such ethnocentricism, it too vanished, and was replaced by an egocentricism the centre of which, however, was not the individual ego, but a greater self.

The Mbuti's quest was for the perfect (effective) sound which it was said, would bring the *molimo* to life, a quest that went on night after night. 'And when ultimately the perfect sound was discovered it coincided with the discovery of the perfect mood: all disharmony, social, spiritual, mental, physical, musical ... all inconsistency ... all incongruity ... vanished and for a brief moment the Mbuti ideal of *ekemi* reigned, 'making good' everything, for, in their own words, whatever *is*, when that moment is reached, is good, otherwise it would not, could not, *be*.'

The Vocal Exercises

These commence with breathing. I use three Shinto breathing exercises which I was taught by my Shiatsu teacher Harriet Geddes. They are invaluable for everyone, from an actor waiting to go on stage to someone awaiting an operation. Indeed Harriet herself taught them to women in a cancer ward whom she had observed lying on their beds, tensed with nerves. The exercises have a deeply calming and centring effect.

One Stand with legs slightly apart so that the feet feel well rooted to the ground like a tree whose roots go deep down. Eyes are closed. As you breathe in, try to visualize the breath commencing at the base of the spine and ascending vertebra by vertebra until it reaches the top of the skull. Here you pause, with your lungs full of breath, resting in the fullness of the breath like a surfboard rider on the crest of a wave. Then you release the breath, you go with the wave, imagining the breath flowing down your face and chest, back to the base of the spine, forming a loop. At this point there is no breath left and you rest now in the emptiness of no-breath. You are neither breathing in nor breathing out. This is a moment which will be familiar to those who do the breath meditation, and recalls those words of Lao Tzu:

> The ten thousand things have their beginning
> In absolute emptiness,
> Complete quiet.
> Energetically growing,
> restlessly changing,
> All complete themselves
> By returning to stillness.

Perform this exercise ten times and then open your eyes and wait quietly until everyone has finished.

Two For the second exercise you visualize the breath flowing up from under the ground, up through the feet, up the back of your ankles, thighs, spine, until it has reached the top of your skull and again you pause, resting in the fullness of the breath, imagining it cascading like a waterfall down your face, chest, down both thighs and legs, into the feet and back into the ground. Again, rest in the emptiness of breath. This exercise takes more concentration. If you find yourself jumping a section, perhaps several of the vertebrae or at the neck, this may well be where you have an area of tension that needs releasing.

   Do this ten times.

Three The third exercise is the same as the second except that now you imagine the breath as it flows up from under the ground, up both legs, up the spine, and to the top of the head, as though it were at a distance of about two inches from the body. When it reaches the top of the skull you imagine it floating there. When you breathe out it is as though you were under a waterfall but just clear of the water itself. It is like putting a shield or a veil about the body, like an aura. You will find this last exercise very powerful.

Again, do it ten times.

Since all sound floats upon the breath we are now ready to work with the voice.

The AH sound You breathe in and then on the exhalation you make an AH sound, keeping the mouth open. Imagine taking a bite of an apple, a large bite, and then relax the muscles of the mouth. Now make the sound. The leader will make a series of different AH sounds: soft, whispered, sighing, loud, short, staccato, laughing, crying. Everyone imitates the leader. This gently flexes the vocal organs. The atmosphere should be playful, not too solemn. Every now and then the sound should be quite vigorous, then followed by soft whispered AHs.

The circling AH Everyone now stands in a circle, hands linked, eyes closed. They begin to sing a sustained AH sound, held on a long breath. The group must keep this going without interruption and without sagging, building the energy and volume of sound, so that it is like a pool of sound, constantly being filled up with the contributions of all present. 'I was amazed by the power of this simple vocal exercise,' wrote one student, 'that long vowel movement of the sustained AH sound, as a unifying force. How just one sound intoned by a group of people can assume such force is beyond me. And when we grouped together, with our eyes closed, it became almost overwhelming.'

When the group is being carried effortlessly by the sound, the leader takes one person by the hand and leads the whole line, hands linked, into a series of spirals (eyes still closed), getting tighter and tighter. Eventually the whole group is so tightly packed together that the individuals within the group can feel the sound resonating in their backs, their thighs, etc. They are possessed by the sound and by its many colours, its many moods. How long this continues is a matter of the leader sensing the energy within the group. There are different ways of ending this exercise. By signalling with a gong or chime the leader can allow the singing gently to subside, or the leader can lead individuals to different parts of the space so that everyone ends up chanting alone. When there is silence everyone should be aware of the resonance continuing. Time is needed for people to relax and lie back, absorbing the experience.

The Song of the Father For this exercise we take the word-sound 'abba', which means both 'the origin of all things', and also 'Daddy'. We sit on the floor cross legged (if comfortable), with eyes closed, and begin to sing the sound 'abba' continuously, without any breaks. We play with the sound, elongating the 'a' sound, and the 'ba' sound, improvising freely. We must feel free to repeat the 'a', 'ba' or 'baba' sounds. We may want to rock forwards and backwards, or to raise our arms in the air, to reach out for 'abba'. We may discover the image of the baby hidden within the father, in the sound 'baba'. We may want and need to stay with that sound and image, being rocked in the arms of the father. Always with eyes closed. Everyone is singing at the same time and the many voices unite as one and yet each singing their own song. We may have feelings related to our own father, or of the father we wished we had had, or of an eternal father. We sing the sound and allow the meaning to take care of itself.

The Song of the Mother If the *Song of the Father* is done in the morning then this should be left till the end of the day, perhaps seated around a candle. They should not be done together. Again, sit cross-legged, eyes closed, elongating the syllables of 'mama' and singing continuously. Interestingly this song usually proves to be the most powerful, and I have known it continue for as long as twenty-five minutes and then fade away into a serene silence. I sometimes imagine a congregation, seated on the floor at evening, singing this *Song of the Mother*. But I doubt that any church would contemplate such a thing. Within the safety and trust of a workshop, however, both these songs have a strong ritualistic effect, as the archetype begins to transcend the autobiographical memories, so that one is carried by the *mana* of the image itself.

The Song of the Name This exercise needs to be done individually. The performer takes her or his own name and improvises an outflowing of continuous sound and movement, letting the sound lead one on a journey into one's real identity.

I have also found that when working with actors on individual roles this exercise, used in connection with a character being played, such as Aase, Peer Gynt's mother, or Marina in *Pericles*, releases layers of unspoken thoughts, feelings and associations.

THE HAND EXERCISES

'Rays flash from his hands; there his power is hidden.'
Habbakuk

Introduction

Look at your hands. They have the power to smash, break and wound. They also have the power to caress, soothe, heal, bless and lift up. They have the power to dig the land, plant seeds, reap crops, operate machinery, bake and cook and serve, dress wounds and perform operations, use musical or technical instruments. They can make furniture, fashion clay, carve stone and wood, weave, sew and embroider, write. They can reach forward in greeting or in dismissal. And embedded in our memories are many such experiences, some painful and humiliating, some joyous and wondrous.

We have two hands, a left and a right, indicating different directions, different possibilities. Even if I am handicapped and have lost a hand, that awareness still remains. The Latin for left is *sinistra*, that which is unknown (hence the word 'sinister'), the unconscious. The Latin for right is *dextra*, leading to the upright, the conscious area of control. To handle something with dexterity means to handle something with conscious knowledge, awareness and skill. We have also the right side of the brain and the left side: one governing the intuitive, creative side of the psyche, and the other the intellectual and rational. We are composed of opposites, of male and female: every woman has within her psyche a male self, which Jung called the *animus*, and every man has in his psyche a female self, which Jung called the *anima*. We find all this in the image of the Tao. We may also recall certain lines of poetry, such as Robert Frost's:

> Two roads diverged in a yellow wood, and I –
> I took the one less travelled by,
> And that has made all the difference.

Hands also remind us of palmistry: on one palm are the lines of life up to the present moment, while on the other hand are the lines of destiny, showing how far and how long we shall travel. A closed hand can be an image of power, of menace, or it may signify a secret as in the children's game when we have to guess which hand contains the pebble or coin.

Before starting the first exercise, remove all rings and watches, and place them somewhere safe.

Hand Ritual for Two People

Kneel on the ground facing your partner, your hands flat on the floor. Kneeling, crouched over, each of you is gazing at four hands.

In the exercise you need to remember two rules. The first is that there is never any eye contact. That is crucial. If you have eye contact you will start relating to each other on a cerebral level and this will inhibit the free flow of exchange and response. By not having eye contact we also achieve a kind of anonymity such as one achieves with the eyes shut or with a blindfold. As the exercise unfolds you are aware of your hands and your partner's hands and of every movement of their body and yours but you never engage the eyes.

The second rule is that you must keep your knees on the ground and you may not move from that spot. Within that limitation the hands are free to go anywhere they want: up, down, behind, to the front, left or right, and where the hands go the body follows, the knees on the ground acting as a hinge. The reason for keeping the knees fixed to the same spot is that without this limitation you would soon be all over the space, and dissipate the intensity of concentration. All ritual implies certain prescribed restraints. These provide the framework.

So there you are, the two of you, kneeling, facing each other. And there are two pairs of hands placed on the ground, and each of you is gazing at these hands, at your own and those of your partner. You remain totally concentrated on the four hands. Suddenly you will experience a feeling response, and the moment this happens you must respond physically, giving that feeling expression through your hands, and the body following wherever the hands may lead, realizing that each hand may operate separately. Thus the left hand might start reaching forward in exploration, while the right hand withdraws behind the back, uncertain and waiting. You might sense some threat from your partner and seek to withdraw, to run away. Or you might feel concern, compassion, for your partner's hands, or curiosity, or a sexual attraction. Whatever the feeling you must not block it, nor edit it, but go with it. Let the hands move. It is like a conversation between two pairs of hands, or a dance. Backwards and forwards go the hands, up and down, circling and swooping, clapping, grasping and releasing, with sharp and stabbing movements, or slow, gentle and caressing. Then suddenly still. You don't have to be moving all the time. But you must engage with your partner through the hands and allow an interaction, an exchange, at a deeper level than that of normal social intercourse. When two strangers do this exercise the power and depth of their encounter can surprise them with its intimacy and trust. It becomes a communing of two spirits.

A small part of you is aware of what is happening, is permitting it. Always you are in control and yet, paradoxically, you are being led. The dance is dancing you. This control is essential as it creates a fundamental basis of trust between the two of you. For example, you might suddenly feel very agressive and violent towards your partner, as though something very deep in you has been aroused and you want to hit out at them, drive them away. You don't hit them, of course, but you do seek a way of expressing through the hands what you are feeling. Instead of wrestling with someone and exhausting yourself or getting caught in a tug-of-war you find strong swift movements to convey the feeling, perhaps even percussive sounds with the hands. In this way neither of you can hurt the other. However strong the feelings aroused you have respect for each other. When you are more familiar with the exercise you will feel like a sculptor shaping space; you will become aware of the relationship of bodies, hands, arms, heads, backs, the ground, the space all round you.

This conversation, or dance, of hands, provided you don't just play 'Pat-a-cake, pat-a-cake', will take you on a journey, and bring you to the end of a phase. With practice you will learn not to break off at this point but both of you will rest in it, aware of the position of the hands (and the body) at that moment of rest, of where you have journeyed. Then, after a time, one of you will feel an impetus to move and so the second phase will commence, and this will take you further into the conversation, deeper into the dance. When you learn to really surrender yourself to the exercise (yet never abandoning yourself), you will find yourself encountering another human being on a deeper level than is usual except in love.

Ritual of Hands for a Group

About nine people is the maximum for this exercise, seven is better. If there is a large number of people then split into a number of groups. All kneel in a circle with hands on the floor forming an inner circle. It is important that no one hurry to make the first move, but wait to gather a group concentration. This variation calls for greater concentration for two reasons. One is that you now have not just one partner but several and so messages are coming from different directions calling for a variety of responses and, therefore, of choices. Secondly, you have to sense when to go with the group and when to remain yourself within the group. If you are too aggressively individualistic it can wreck the group, but also if one follows the group too slavishly, the energy will peter out. There has to be a sensitive giving and receiving, acting and responding, so that, with confidence, several patterns can spring up interweaving with one another. When the exercise is really under way then everyone is wholly absorbed, caught up, in the group dynamism, so that to those outside watching, it is like watching the organic development of root, stem and flower. Once the exercise reaches its conclusion everyone should lie back, relaxing, thinking over the many images. This should then be followed by each group having its own discussion as to what images and themes were emerging, and how these might be developed further.

The Solo Hand Ritual

Again kneel on one spot and focus on the hands until one or both move. We have to go where the hands take us, and yet it is never movement for movement's sake or making pretty aesthetic movements. Like keeping a journal, one is communing with oneself. The exercise had its genesis for me in a dance work which I saw performed in New York by the modern dancer Sybil Shearer; it was entitled *Seven Images of An Answer*. The first image commenced with the dancer seated on the floor and only the hands moving, reaching out from side to side, above and below, in a pondering search, as though probing the space immediately round the body. Slowly the dancer rose, the hands mounting one above the other, reaching high up, cutting and slicing space. Suddenly the hands dropped, falling away, as though chasms were opening before her and abysses of darkness had been revealed. The work ended with the dancer once again seated, cross-legged, and now, for the first time, the hands came together, palm to palm, as though the answer lay in prayer. I was reminded of Wordsworth's lines from *The Prelude*:

> Those obstinate questionings
> Of sense and outward things,
> Fallings from us, vanishings,
> Blank misgivings of a creature
> Moving about in worlds not realised,
> High instincts before which our mortal nature
> Did tremble like a guilty thing surprised.

Each of the hand exercises can be performed either in silence or accompanied by a steady drumbeat. Melodic or strongly rhythmic music should never be used as it will only impose itself on the performers. I sometimes use Zen music for meditation, or other Japanese music which does not have familiar associations or rhythms for Westerners.

The solo hand exercise can also be used with older or handicapped people, seated on chairs.

From Anita's Journal It was in the solo hand exercise that I first experienced a strong overwhelming image and allowed myself to go with it. Even as I write now, I can still sense the feeling I had that my right hand was male and my left female and that no matter whether they're working together or in opposition, the movement of one affects the other. I was so excited that something 'worked' for me! [Some days later:]
The solo hand exercise which I did today brought on an entirely different set of images than had the first time. I was all prepared to be open for my hands to be male or female, but they couldn't seem to care less! All the images that came to me had to do with shape and space, and how movement can form shape. Most of the time my hands were curved either inwards or outwards, and moved always in a curved or circular motion. Only once was I prompted to draw angles in the air. For the first time, too, repetition was important. I wanted to swing my hands over and over in the same arc, going just a bit further each time, until the momentum carried my arms around in a complete circle – what a moment! The world seemed full of the simple joy of swinging my arms!

On reflection this joy may be that I had completed a shape – something had closure – I had defined space. James remarked how this may have something to do with my need to find a space in my new environment. Even though I have been here over two years I have always had the feeling that since it is only a temporary stop I have no real roots here. This year is much more stable, but the first two years I was miserable. It's ironic that I'm beginning to identify my space – and be secure in my identity – in my final year here. I'm thinking of developing a ritual of welcome and reacquaintance. My fiancé lives seven hours away and as he is in grad. school as well, we don't see each other very often. Usually it takes me at least an entire day and night to get used to someone else suddenly being in my personal space. Perhaps a ritual would help ease this time. Because the hand-washing ritual, when we did it, helped decrease the fear of touch, that might be worked in. I want to share the dance for two pairs of hands with him as well. I'll work on it because I need something to help me centre down at this transitional time.

From Lori's Journal The hand exercise was a wonderful subconscious outpouring of what has been happening to me lately. I started out with the feeling that my hands wanted freedom, but a crushing weight was forcing me to use my hands to push and hold this weight off the rest of my body. I felt the weight on my hands and through my arms and back. I pushed and pushed to no avail. I decided to stop pushing. The weight stopped, and I floated out of it. I felt as though I had freed myself. I began to close myself in – protecting myself in a bubble – but this became claustrophobic and I crashed out of this suffocating bubble. And then the sense of freedom was restored. My hands became still. This had a profound effect upon me.

A BEREAVEMENT RITUAL

It is best for this to be done in the afternoon of a day workshop, using the time before it to explore images of journeying. A space of two hours should be set aside for the exercise itself and there must be no pressure at the end for people to leave the building. It must be allowed to take as much time as it needs, as well as for the participants to be able to earth themselves before leaving the workshop area and environment. There is no music.

A round basket or dish of balls of coloured wool is placed in the centre of the space and everyone forms a large circle around it. Each participant is invited to think of someone they know who has died. When each feels ready then each steps forward to pick up a ball of wool, the colour of which may remind them of the person they are commemorating. On returning to the perimeter of the circle, the loose end of the wool is wound a few times around a finger of the left hand, while the ball is held in the right hand. While waiting for everyone to pick up a ball of wool, each is reflecting on the person's life. When everyone is ready – but there must be no hurry – someone may throw their ball across the circle to someone else, whose eye they have caught. This throwing of the balls of wool across the circle, which is what creates a giant circular tapestry, *must not be hurried*. Everything must proceed at a meditative pace. The throwing of the balls is itself a meditation.

On catching a ball, the recipient winds a few strands of the wool around a finger of the left hand, and then throws the ball on to someone else. As the spinning gets under way, each participant gets caught up in the lives of others, with many different coloured threads wound about their left hand. Soon, coloured balls are flying in various directions, weaving in and out of the tapestry. If a ball lands on the floor and no one can reach it then the leader of the group must step in and retrieve it, handing it to the person to whom it had been thrown. The atmosphere should be concentrated and at the same time relaxed. Each participant is aware of the game of throwing and catching and weaving, while at the same time recalling memories of the person who has died, and seeing their life and death in relation to all these other lives and deaths. It is possible that one person may start to sing. Others may choose to join in, or not.

Eventually, when the tapestry is beginning to sag, and almost everyone in the circle has used up their wool, the leader will move slowly round the outside of the circle and with a pair of strong scissors cut off the ends of wool nearest the left hand of each person, leaving each individual holding many coloured strands of wool. This cutting needs great sensitivity on the part of the leader. He or she must avoid eye contact and yet be very aware of each person. Even though warned in advance that this is going to happen, nonetheless it always comes as a shock and in some can unleash tears not shed until that moment.

How the exercise develops beyond this point, when the tapestry lies collapsed in the centre, a tangle of wool, and each person is left with a posy of coloured threads, depends upon the group and the individuals within it. This is why the exercise must remain

open-ended, without any pressure to finish it. The conclusion
awaits. For a long time, apart from individual reactions, it may
appear as though nothing is going to happen. Sometimes it can
seem as though everyone has abandoned themselves to an impossible grief. Only rarely will a group, like the community of
nuns described in Chapter 7, find their way surely and inexorably
towards a conclusion. Usually this only happens when the group
has a shared ethos, or has worked together over a period of time.
More usually, any group of individuals in our Western society,
drawn from many different backgrounds, when faced with the
nakedness of grief, the finality of death, are bereft; and at the same
time know that there can be no easy, sentimental drawing together
of the threads. And so one waits, trusting to the creative process to
throw up an image or a sound which will resonate and lead the
ritual forward to its unique conclusion, unique for that group at
that moment.

'I stood before a dark cave, waiting to go in,' was the dream of a
patient at the start of her analysis, 'and I shuddered at the thought
that I might not be able to find my way back.' The journey into our
own interior landscape always involves a risk, but none more so
than in this particular exercise. This is how Scott Phillips, a PhD
student at Ohio State University in Columbus described the
experience.

FROM SCOTT'S JOURNAL

The group stands in a circle, each one holding a ball of yarn. The
exercise is one of helping the participant to come to terms with the
letting go of a friend or family member who has died. The participants are invited to think of the deceased, someone who has died
and to whom they feel close. If anyone has not had the experience
of losing someone close to them, they are invited to consider the
death of someone close to them who is still alive, or even their own
death. At such a time as anyone feels moved to do so, they are to
toss their ball of yarn to anyone else in the group, all the while
holding one end of the yarn wrapped around their finger. This
tossing and wrapping continues until an intricate yarn tapestry

has been woven, made from the various crossings of different-coloured yarn. At some point, as the yarn supply is about to exhaust itself, a designated person circumnavigates the circle snipping the strands of yarn that connect each participant to the tapestry. At this point whatever happens is allowed to happen. The participants are instructed to maintain the imagery of the loved one throughout the exercise. After I had been separated from the tapestry, I discovered that small candles had been placed around the outside of the circle.

I loved this exercise. At first I associated my ball of yarn with the person I was recalling. I stood for a long time holding the yarn, feeling its texture, nuzzling it, all the while recalling memories of my experiences with this person. When I initially tossed my first ball of yarn I felt as if that was the moment of symbolic separation. As the tapestry grew bigger and more complex, however, I began to associate this person with the tapestry as a whole and I did not feel that I had actually been separated as yet. For the time being I still felt her presence. As the exercise, which was rather lengthy, continued, I could see how it was affecting people in different ways. Some began to weep openly, while others seemed lost in silent meditation. I never felt overwhelmed by emotion; I felt as if I had already said goodbye and made my closure with this person and therefore there was no emotional urge to repeat it. I was filled, however, with a sense of longing and sadness as well as a warm feeling constituted by fond memories. The most emotional moment for me was when I was forced to separate from the tapestry. This was the moment of symbolic separation. After being left alone with bits of yarn still wrapped around my fingers, I found a candle and began to untangle these bits of yarn. For some reason I felt this need to untangle the yarn and arrange each strand before the candle, as though it were some sort of shrine. I noticed that most people had gravitated to a candle and most were doing something with the yarn. Somehow the final moments, each of us at our own candle, constituted a final closure; for me it lay in the systematic arrangement of the yarn, for others it was something else.

Evidently some people did not feel as enthusiastic about the exercise as I did. Some did not wish to grieve over someone they had already grieved over, others were distracted from their thoughts by the mechanics of throwing and catching the yarn. As for the first objection I saw no reason why this had necessarily to be a grieving exercise in the sense that one would always end up experiencing a gut-wrenching, weepy catharsis. The feelings I had were mostly celebratory, although they were tinged with sadness. I felt quite good about the feelings I experienced and rejoiced in the fact that I had been a part of this person's life. The second objection was more understandable, although the mechanics of the yarn-throwing was the activity which could actually free my mind to meditate more effectively. The act of weaving became a rhythm which helped channel my concentration. I did not see the activity as a distraction, but as a part of the meditation itself.

I could see this exercise being used in hospices with terminally ill people participating. It might serve as a way to help the dying come to terms with their own death.

THE BAMBOO POLES EXERCISE

Bamboo poles are better than wooden ones because they have more spring in them, and taper to one end. However, if bamboo is not available then wooden poles can be used. They should be about 8–9 feet in length. They should be of a width such as the performer can hold within his hand. About five to seven poles should be used. The actor has to assemble them in one bundle, in any position or angle, and imagine that they are antennae, extensions of his own limbs, that he was born with them or that they are burdens to be carried through life.

I first explored this exercise with a young actor at the National Theatre in Helsinki, Jaarko Tamminen. He chose to enter with one pole across his back and his arms looped over it and his eyes closed – like the blinded Oedipus. As he travelled, his feet touched pole after pole lying on the ground. Gradually he gathered all these poles, struggling to hold them in his arms, the poles slipping and sliding. Then, swiftly, with a determined movement, he seized them together into one bundle and in his excitement raced around the hall, his eyes suddenly opened. But at this moment he lost control of the poles, which slithered to the floor with a great clatter, and he collapsed prostrate on the ground. Slowly he reached forward his hand towards one pole, realizing now that he must tackle one problem at a time. His response reminded me of Robert Frost's poem, 'The Armful':

> For every parcel I stoop down to seize,
> I lose some other off my arms and knees,
> And the whole pile is slipping, bottles, buns,
> Extremes too hard to comprehend at once,
> Yet nothing I should care to leave behind.
> With all I have to hold with, hand and mind,
> And heart if need be, I will do my best
> To keep their building balanced at my breast.
> I crouch down to prevent them as they fall;
> Then sit down in the middle of them all.
> I had to drop the armful in the road
> And try to stack them in a better load.

The poles serve as a starting point to stimulate images in a stream of consciousness arising from the unconscious of each individual. One PhD Student from India, Kaizaad Kotwal, found his response to this exercise enormously enriching, as the poles became first a raft, then oars with which to paddle his way upstream, then weapons with which to defend himself against an attack from assailants on all sides, and finally a shrine over which to pray after successfully defeating his 'enemies'. All this was unpremeditated, the form coming entire in the first session, reaching its own conclusion and forming a ritualizing of his own situation in America, thousands of miles away from his home, isolated in a new college, very much on his own. The following day he was able to repeat it before his peers one of whom, Roger Freeman, wrote as follows.

FROM ROGER'S JOURNAL

Intriguing things today. Kaizaad worked a 'ritual-in-progress', involving long bamboo poles, that touched me as relating to many of the concerns I've been coming to grips with these last few weeks, that nasty question of how one establishes one's place in alien surroundings. I suspect much that informs the ritual he has been working on with James relates to his move to the States from India, just as my perception of it is based on my move from the West.

In the ritual he embarked on a journey (with the poles), just as I have done, to a foreign land where he had to define his place in an initially hostile environment. Surrounded on all sides by hostile forces, he reacted (understandably) defensively, marking his territory and asserting his power within the arena he occupied. It was a very positive experience to see him begin to feel comfortable in his surroundings and to exult in his personal accomplishment. And within this new land he found a personal spiritual bond that apparently gave him a great feeling of 'belongingness'. (All this with a few bamboo poles!) I hope I will be able to find such a bond here, though I doubt it can possibly be as strong as the one I feel to Home. Which is all right; it's nice to know where you come from.

Perhaps the most moving example of this exercise as a rite of passage is the experience of a student at Middlesex Polytechnic in London.

FROM PAUL'S JOURNAL

Monday the 10th was one of the days that sticks out most for me in the five-week period of working with James. It was the day I worked with the bamboo poles. I was told to use them as though they were part of me, as though I had lived with them always, and I was told to travel, to go on a journey with them. At first no image came to my mind and so I waited patiently as we had been taught to do. Then, all of a sudden, a picture of my mother flashed into my mind. She has suffered from Parkinson's disease for twenty years and as a child I had grown up submerged in my mother's illness. Now, in this room, with these crutches made out of bamboo, I was transformed into a cripple. For the first time I knew exactly what she felt like. Trapped and yet not trapped. Unable to walk as others did and yet with the power to move. Like being caught in a slow-moving nightmare which you cannot wake up from because you are already awake. Yet each day it becomes that little bit harder to walk. A little more effort is needed to do certain things until the power to do these specific things goes and recedes into the blackness of cruel memory. I think if I have one fear in life it is to end my days as my mother is still doing. Locked in a mobility vacuum, a slow motion film that is slowly, almost imperceptibly, running down. A life that is no life, a death that is no death. This I fear and yet it has taken me all this time to come to terms with my own emotions. *Until that day in New Hall when I faced them finally.*

Just as the purpose of education is not merely to increase the quantity of knowledge and information, important though this may be, but to deepen and enrich the quality of life itself, so, too, in ritual the aim must be to bring people into communion with those mysterious forces of vitality and meaning that lie within them.

THE FRONTIER EXERCISE

'Now. When I have overcome my fears — of others, of myself, of the underlying darkness:
at the frontier of the unheard-of.
Here ends the known. But from a source beyond it,
something fills my being with its possibilities —
At the frontier.'

Dag Hammarskjold, *Markings*

The purpose of this exercise was explained in Chapter 2, but the following passage from Paul Auster's most recent novel, *Moon Palace*, vividly expresses its essence. 'I walked without interruption, heading towards the Pacific, borne along by a growing sense of happiness. Once I reached the end of the continent, I felt that some important question would be resolved for me. I had no idea what that question was, but the answer had already been formed in my steps, and I had only to keep walking to know that I had left myself behind, that I was no longer the person I had once been.'

The frontier is marked out at one end of the space with rope or poles laid end to end. Three-quarters of the space should be left for the journey itself, and the final quarter for the other side of the frontier. After an initial discussion about the image of the frontier, it is helpful to commence with some physical exercises which involve different ways of travelling to it before actually attempting the exercise.

One by one the following sequence is explored: slow walking, foot after foot; rolling over; crawling on one's belly; hopping; and any other variations that occur to those taking part. If I stress the physical it is because there is a form of knowledge which is beyond words or the intellect. We may talk for ever in a seminar, or in analysis, about the concept of pilgrimage or ritual, but it is only through *doing*, through the experience itself, that we can gain those necessary insights which may result in a true rite of passage.

From Sandra's Journal As I was readying to begin the journey to the frontier I felt an affliction, something holding me back. I turned it into an image of a wounded foot which I had to carry to the frontier. I was quite determined. It was difficult to drag my leg all that way, but I did it, and I never considered turning back because it seemed so important that I reach the frontier. And when I did it was healed! For me it wasn't what I'd reached that healed me but the fact that I'd completed the journey. James suggested that I consider what the wounded leg represented, what weakness in myself. Perhaps it represents my fear of moving forwards. If I could carry that fear and press it on with me as I go, make it a reason to go further, then when I reach my destination it will have been cured. If I nurture the fear and let it rest where it wants to stay it will only grow and cripple me. This is the idea in embryo, and I hope that before long in my life I'll be able to locate and define this weakness and carry it over the necessary frontier. It was a very long, rich morning.

Travelling to the Frontier with a Burden

One variant of the exercise is to perform it in pairs, with one person representing a burden that the traveller has to carry with them. In real life we all have burdens of one kind or another: the burden of aged or infirm parents, a handicapped child or partner, guilt or fear, and so on. For one man in his forties, married with a family, it was this exercise in particular which illuminated his marriage, as he himself subsequently wrote.

> All of the exercises touched me in some way or another, but one has informed me more than the rest, and revealed something I know I would never have reached in any other way. You asked us to journey to the frontier with a burden. Joseph Campbell said of marriage that 'most people expect it to be a long love affair and it isn't. Marriage is an ordeal. It has nothing to do with being happy. It has to do with being transformed.' I was helped by him to understand my own marriage as an instrument for transformation. In doing the exercise, in journeying to the frontier with a burden, I had myself tied to Iris [one of the other participants in the workshop], who was to pull in the opposite direction. She did this impossibly well! The extreme effort might have called forth my considerable rageful anger but, instead, and in a way I couldn't have experienced through my intellect, I found myself being very tender with my burden, patiently suc-cumbing to its responsibilities, and tenderly lifting the burden along, taxing all my strength – when, finally, the opposition yielded a little. This has opened in me an awareness which I believe will help me enormously. I am quite sure that this exer-cise has etched a channel of understanding in me along which an energy will flow to good effect when the 'ordeal' is tough. 'Ordeal: a severe trial, a test by fire.' Those few minutes and the length of a room have furnished me with an experience of moving through an ordeal and established a paradigm of unusual force.

THE SCROLL OF LIFE

Each individual has a roll of white lining paper which is unrolled to a length of 30–40 feet, and fixed at either end with weights or drawing pins. A double thickness of newspaper should be placed under the scroll so that the paint used in this exercise cannot seep through, while at the far end there should be a mat of newspaper so that on completion of the walk the participants can wash and dry their feet. Mix poster paint with water in plastic bowls, each bowl containing a different colour. The mixture should be neither too runny nor too thick. If the space being used for the workshop is wide enough then several scrolls can be laid side to side, allowing a space of about 3 feet between each. In this way several people can set out on their journeys simultaneously.

Each traveller chooses a colour, dips his or her feet in the paint, and commences to make 'footprints in the sands of time' as they walk along the scroll. Each traveller also has a companion for the journey who will travel alongside, on the 3-foot passageway to one side of the scroll. The task of the companion is wait upon the traveller's needs, holding the bowl of paint in readiness for when the traveller needs to dip his or her feet into the paint (which tends to dry off fairly quickly), and also to see that they do not slip in the wet paint, especially when balancing on one leg before putting down the other foot onto the paper to make a print.

This calligraphy of the feet is Zen-like in its simplicity and beauty, which does not mean that it is simple. The cynical can choose to walk from one end to the other and say: 'So what?' For the exercise to be Zen-like, and achieve the quality of a ritual, each traveller must first centre down, and stand gazing at the length of the journey ahead. The scroll represents one's life journey and as the journey unfolds so will one's response. I repeat: the exercise is only meaningful if one is centred. One can cheat but the only person one cheats is oneself. On completion of the journey the traveller looks back on the way he or she has come; then, after washing and drying their feet, they will return quietly to the starting point to contemplate their scroll of life.

The scrolls need to be hung up to dry and usually each person wants to take their scroll home.

THE ROPE EXERCISES

Active/Passive

You require white lengths of rope, of the softness and flexibility that one finds in an upholsterer's store, about a quarter of an inch in thickness. The ends of the rope should be knotted to form a circle. An even number of participants space themselves around the rope, standing in a circle. The leader names every other person 'active', and those in between 'passive'. At the stroke of a drum-beat those who are active take one strong move, holding the rope taut, while those who are 'passive' respond by yielding and taking up whatever position they move or fall into, also keeping the rope taut. Only one move is allowed, not two or three. Everyone should then freeze into this position and wait for the next drum-beat. It is important that everyone is aware of the patterns being created by the rope and the bodies and to sense the inner connections. Everyone should be encouraged to explore the space and not just stand upright in a circle, and the feet can also be used to control the rope. After a while the leader announces: 'Now the "passives" become "actives" and the "actives" become "passives".' And so on.

This simple exercise teaches everyone how to manipulate the rope (keeping it taut is essential, using hands, feet, arms, even teeth), creating different patterns and relationships, sculpting in space.

The Journey

Following on from this, groups of seven take the rope and go to one end of the working space, and imagine that they are going on a journey to an unknown destination or frontier. Now they are not given designated roles, but must respond as they see fit, choosing for themselves, from moment to moment, whether to be active or passive. For the first two or three attempts it is helpful if the leader controls the exercise with a drum-beat. On each drum-beat the participants move and then freeze until the next drum-beat. Without this initial control the whole exercise becomes frenetic and the rope tangled. The exercise continues until everyone has arrived at the end of the space, completing the journey or voyage.

Inevitably, in the first attempt or two, everyone becomes 'active' so that a lot of aggression is released and there is a risk that the exercise becomes a tug-of-war and everyone ends up being exhausted. There is a tendency for everyone to rush the exercise, and not allow enough time to absorb the various images that are unfolding and to find responses to them. As the group becomes more familiar with the exercise and aware of its potential, so it grows in richness, and there is a deeper awareness of meetings and partings, or someone collapsing on the journey and the whole group having to drag or carry that person; or the leadership may change *en route*. This exercise, used with young people, is also richly instructive in the importance of interrelationships.

The Birth-Maturity-Ageing-Death-Rebirth Exercise

This exercise I owe to that remarkable man, Ken Feit, who called himself the Itinerant Fool, and who travelled the world leading workshops.

There should be no more than seven to nine people on the rope (still in the form of a circle), and there should be a distance of about 4 feet between each individual. This exercise, like all the other exercises, must be done in bare feet. Everyone takes hold of the rope and lies down, imagining that they are not yet born. At all times they must maintain contact with the rope, using their feet, hands, teeth, or some other part of the body, and keeping the rope taut. If the rope is not kept taut it will become tangled and the exercise will come to a halt. Throughout the exercise eyes are kept closed – this is essential.

There they lie, imagining themselves not yet born. Some may choose to curl up in a foetus position. Then, in movement but no sound, they imagine being born, learning to walk, growing up, growing older, dying and being dead. When they have 'died' they have a choice: to remain dead or to be reborn. Everyone is on their own and yet, as the exercise unfolds, may bump into someone else: chance meetings and then partings. The individual must respond to whatever images arise, as well as to unexpected developments. Thus one person might be standing upright, dancing and exulting in their maturity, when suddenly the pressure of the rope from either side may drag them down, causing them to collapse. They may imagine that they have been struck down by an illness, from which they may recover, or which may result in an early 'death'.

Again, this may not be death in the physical sense but, represent rather the death of an ambition or a relationship.

The exercise should be allowed all the time it needs – at the very least half an hour, but it can go on much longer. To those watching, the shifting patterns of people and ropes is often of startling beauty and very moving, beyond the imaginings of any choreographer, and all this achieved by people with their eyes closed. It is a remarkable fact that with their eyes closed people's imaginations are set free from any censoring or inhibition; while movement can be free and vigorous without any accidents. Very large or overweight people are seen to move with delicacy and grace, as though suddenly released.

At the end the leader should invite those who have done the exercise to lie back and, still with closed eyes, think back over the journey they have taken. Since the exercise takes people to surprising depths this period of reflection must not be hurried. It can then be followed by a period of sharing experiences.

From Anita's Journal The group rope exercise was the most successful prolonged activity in which I have participated. From the instant I closed my eyes to the instant I opened them I remained focused and image after image flew through my head. The rope became my world – I was inside, outside, underneath, standing on – always somehow conscious of my relation to the rope. It was also *my* world. I got very claustrophobic about it when someone else entered it, and it recalls my remark earlier, à propos my fiancé: 'It usually takes me an entire day and night to get used to someone else suddenly being in my personal space.'

THE WASHING RITUAL

Introduction

While it is impossible to be dogmatic about time, this particular exercise should last about an hour; if it is hurried it will achieve nothing. Within Christian churches there is a fear of taking time and making spaces for silence. As one mature student observed,

'One of the things which afflicts American religion is its own impatience to be done with itself. The imperative to be done within an hour is detrimental to a real experience of worship. Where is the time for corporate meditation and reflection? I often wish that, in place of the homily which is usually too long and almost always banal, there could be a twenty-minute period of absolute silent meditation.'

Our feet in Western society are kept stockinged, socked and bound in tight shoes, and women's posture is often severely damaged by high heels. Imprisoned within shoes our feet grow flat, stiff and inflexible, and are punished by corns. It is only when we have some accident to our feet that we realize how dependent we are upon them to carry the whole weight of the body. Our feet are the point at which we experience our connection with the ground that supports us; it is where we feel that we are 'rooted', as in the Shinto breathing exercises. The foot is also a delicate and complicated piece of equipment, made up of twenty-six separate bones. Even more importantly there are tens of thousands of nerve endings in the sole of the foot, and the opposite ends of these nerves are located over the rest of the body. The foot is a map of the entire body. There is no muscle, gland or organ in the body without a set of nerves whose opposite ends are anchored in the foot, so that when the foot is massaged the rest of the body is affected. From this observation there has developed the practice of zone therapy or reflexology as it is also called.

The image of feet suggests strength. Feet can stamp on, crush and dominate. 'To put one's foot down' implies an attitude of firmness, of declaring one's stamp – as in the Scroll of Life exercise. There also appears to be something in the human psyche that can inspire us to prostrate ourselves before the feet of another person, or to kiss the foot of a sacred statue. There are foot fetishists, but also natural erotic associations with the foot. The naked foot is often disturbing to many people, suggesting perhaps an unleashed animality. It is a curious fact that Jesus's command to his disciples at the Last Supper to wash one another's feet is today virtually ignored, with the exception of a rather perfunctory enactment during Holy Week in certain religious houses. One has to ask why.

Images of feet occur in people's dreams and, of course, in mythology. We speak of idols having feet of clay, while Oedipus's weakness lies in his feet which were pierced as a baby when he was thrown out into the wilderness by his mother to die. Similarly the feet (and hands) of Christ are wounded, an image which recurs in Arthurian legend in the story of the Fisher King whose feet never heal. We also have such expressions as: to shoot oneself in the foot; to put one's foot down; lame duck; to put one's foot in it; always one foot on the ground, one foot in the grave, 'footfalls echo in the memory'; 'He will not suffer thy foot to be moved'; 'and did those feet in ancient time'; 'the feet of him that bringeth good tidings'; and so on.

It will be found that a group discussion will produce many images and also personal associations. Following such a discussion, certain preliminary exercises will help prepare the way for the main exercise which is that of washing the feet.

Preliminary Exercises

Everyone lies on their back with feet and hands in the air. Music (some Bach or Mozart, Corelli or Vivaldi) is played. Each person creates a dance with their hands and feet, responding to the music.

Now everyone breaks up into pairs. Each couple lies back, buttocks to buttocks, and relates to the other through the feet, caressing, pushing, touching, creating a dance of the feet. Hands may also be used.

Homage to Feet Exercise Everyone forms up into two lines, each line facing the other, but with a distance of about 20 feet between each line. A steady drum-beat accompanies this exercise.

The first row advances towards the other, each person focusing their attention upon the feet of their opposite number. On approaching close to, everyone in the first line lies prostrate before the feet of the person opposite them, and caresses, touches, licks, or responds in any way that they are moved to do. All this must be done slowly, meditatively, while the person whose feet are being acknowledged in this way must accept what is happening, and not respond physically. Eventually the person paying homage stands up, steps back a pace, makes a deep obeisance, and returns to the starting point. The exercise is then repeated for the other line.

The Washing Exercise

After these preliminary exercises, each individual is blindfolded, led to a different part of the room and linked up with a partner, but neither will know who the other is. They kneel or sit cross-legged. They begin to caress and explore each other's hands (minus rings, watches and bracelets), trying to sense the other person through touch. After about ten minutes, the leader places a bowl between each pair, with a towel at the side of each person. The hands are guided towards the bowl. Water is now poured into the bowls from a height, splashing over the hands, the sound of the water increasing in depth as the bowls are filled. Music is played, but nothing traditional or melodic – preferably Japanese, music suitable for meditation.

Once the hands have been washed – and all this is done very slowly, meditatively – each pair proceeds to wash each other's feet, and to dry them. It is important that this should take as long as is needed. It sounds very simple but it is in fact an exercise that has a deep resonance, and stirs people. Once, at Grand Rapids in Michigan, one couple went on much longer than the rest and so the blindfolds of the rest were removed, and everyone sat in a circle around the couple who were still washing each other, as though present at a betrothal. It is as though the exercise arouses archaic memories, and time falls away.

It takes time to bring people down to earth after such an intensity of sharing and communion. When the blindfolds are removed, the couples sit looking at each other. Finally, everyone is brought into a circle for any comments or feedback. Some will be too moved to speak. That is all right. No one should be expected to speak for the sake of speaking. Sometimes, as Shakespeare wrote, 'Silence is the perfect'st herald of joy.' As one participant remarked of this exercise: 'Foot-washing really *is* an act of humility. I never really had given it that much thought until I actually experienced it.'

THE NEWSPAPER WORKSHOP

This needs a whole day. Everyone arrives with a large pile of newspapers and magazines, some reels of adhesive tape 1 inch wide, and a pair of scissors. The morning's task is for everyone to create a fantastic costume, with head-dress and mask, to completely cover each person. Everyone must work separately without talking, each centring down into their own creativity. Help may be asked from neighbours when it comes to putting on the costumes at the end of the morning. Music is played.

This workshop reveals a rich variety of creativity, releasing a high degree of energy. Time is forgotten, and often three hours is not enough time. The ingenuity of design, of construction, is always amazing. Very quickly people learn the simple techniques: to use two of three layers of paper rather than one, which can tear too easily. After three hours everyone dons their costume and there is a parade so that everyone has a chance to see the results. Sometimes pairs are formed, and a simple ceremonial evolves, or a puppet-like play, the various 'characters' fitting into a folk tale. Lastly the leader, carrying perhaps a big drum, will lead everyone out into the streets in procession. The response on people's faces is often a bonus to the morning's work. Tired or bored or self-enclosed people are suddenly taken out of themselves at the unexpected sight and gaiety of the procession.

The afternoon session focuses on a group creation of a 'God' figure, built out of newspaper on a single person. It begins with a discussion of what we think we mean by 'God', what our expectations are, what people in other cultures and other times have thought or felt 'God' to be, and what our expectations or feelings are. Everyone will have a different idea, which is natural since 'God', if there be a God, must be beyond all knowing, both male and female. All our ideas of 'God' are but pictures, images, an attempt to 'know' God. Images of God as mother, father, leader, child, holy man or woman, god, goddess, emptiness, energy, will emerge.

Then one person is invited to volunteer to be the 'God' figure. Since this role is physically and emotionally exhausting it needs explaining beforehand. The figure has to 'suffer' other people's projections, and carry the weight of their expectations. He or she is someone who carries our burdens as well as our projections. The volunteer will have to stand in the centre of the space, with arms upheld to the sides, and be quite still for possibly as long as an hour, while the rest create their image of 'God' to impose on him or her. At the start, because of the strain on the arms it is possible to use some kind of support such as two up-ended brooms. The volunteer must gaze ahead, and be absolutely centred. The rest sit about among the piles of newspapers, pondering what to make. Slowly they start making objects; perhaps a crown or a mask for the head, or a halo or sun-burst; others may create armlets, gloves, elongated fingers to put over the fingers of the person. It is always amazing how everyone works as an ensemble, complementing what each is doing. Some will stand back just watching and then, moved by an impulse or an idea, will start to fashion their contribution or to build on what someone else has started. Slowly the whole figure is covered and the identity of the volunteer disappears under the projections of the group. At some point the crutches supporting the arms are removed.

Once again, as in the morning's session, people's own creativity carries them along on its own momentum. When the figure is created, others may start to clear the space around, creating a kind of *temenos* or temple, and then all sit, quite spontaneously, to gaze at what they have created, their own idol or image of 'God'. Others may come forward to hang a votive offering on the figure. At one workshop a Jungian analyst spent all her time in a corner quietly cutting, sticking and making a votive offering. When the figure was completed she stepped forward and fastened it to the front of the figure. It was a large heart, made of several thicknesses of paper, onto which she had fixed, cut from magazines and colour supplements, many faces of young and old people, men, women and children: a heart of all mankind and womankind. As she hung it on the figure she burst into deep tears, caught wholly by surprise by the intensity of her own emotion at that moment.

Everyone sits round waiting, watching. Again, as in the bereavement ritual, no one knows what will happen. If we believe in this 'God', what will we do next? What do we want to do? Similarly if we do not believe in it, either partially or wholly, what will we do now? We have to find in sound and movement some way of expressing our response. Out of this the drama of the ritual will develop. And what of the 'God' figure? It may be that he or she will move first; if so, what is motivating them? Being incarcerated inside an elaborate newspaper costume, often unable to see, their movement will of necessity be slow and stylized, ritualized. Nothing, or everything may happen. However the exercise resolves itself it is crucial that it be gently grounded and earthed. And if 'the god' is still inside the costume then everyone should help gently disrobe 'him' and enable the individual to 'come down to earth'. Sometimes, often, the exercise reaches a violent and destructive climax of adulation turning into hate: Long live the King! The King must die! When the figure is destroyed, it may be rebuilt, or a male god figure replaced by a female one. Whatever transpires, there must be plenty of time for sharing and discussion. Finally the group should be invited to find a simple ritual of their own for ending the day. Sometimes this is achieved by the practical necessity of gathering up all the paper and putting it into large polythene bags. This clearing process often results in a carnival-like atmosphere of laughter and songs.

THE CANDLE EXERCISE

'I shall light a candle of understanding in thine heart, which shall not be put out.'

The Book of Esdras

In many ways this is best done at the end of a day's workshop when darkness is gathering (or can be created by closing blinds or shutters). People are tired, yet stimulated, relaxed and open.

All sit in a circle around a candle, gazing at its flame, absorbing the experience. When the leader senses the moment is right, those present are invited to express the images which the candle suggests to them. Someone will observe how vulnerable the candle flame is to every draught, how easily blown out; another will remark how the small flame emphasizes the surrounding darkness, and the danger 'out there'; someone else may stress the flame serving as a focal point in the darkness, like a lantern, drawing everyone to its centre. Other images will occur: that while the candle is giving light and warmth it is at the same time eating itself up; in burning it is burning itself up. Tiny though the flame is, it can provide warmth, a means of energy, of cooking, and yet at the same time it can destroy, set a whole forest on fire: it can illuminate but it can also destroy. All these images and associations add up to the many-faceted symbol of the candle, and the exercise demonstrates how a symbol is so much more than an image. Jung, in reference to symbols, observed: 'Their pregnant language cries out to us that they mean more than they can say.'

After an interval of silence the leader may blow out the candle or else invite everyone to blow until the flame is extinguished. Now all sit in the darkness, absorbing this experience of no-light, of a void, blindness, blackness, death. The leader then passes candles, one for each person, and relights the central candle. From this flame everyone present lights their own candle until there is a pool of flames. Again, people may want to share their thoughts and feelings and associations. A procession may form, and singing. It is a good moment for the *Song of the Mother*.

Epilogue

'That was the real world: I have touched it once
And now I shall know it always.'

Edwin Muir

For all who commit themselves to these exercises there is always this experience of having touched the real world. The process cannot but be therapeutic, deepening our insights, while for some it will become a rite of passage, effecting a fundamental transformation in the lives of those concerned. The creative process enables us to absorb experience with our whole being, to give it a form and shape, thereby enhancing our capacity to live. By gaining conscious control of unconscious imagery we bring into order our own chaotic psyches. It is a process of self-healing. As Anna Halprin once remarked to me, 'Art is an enduring process, for it touches on the spiritual dimension in a way that no other human activity does. In art you are able to give expression to that which lies deep inside you and, having given expression to it, you receive back a vision which is a map by which you can set your other goals.'

The use of the word 'art' raises another possibility for the exercises. Although the histrionic is a natural tendency – when we are happy we sing and dance, when we are frustrated we stamp and swear, when in pain we rock and moan – nonetheless, although these actions can afford temporary relief, the histrionic is not art, for art implies a form and shape in time and space and the necessity of communicating its contents to others so that it can become a shared experience. Anthony O'Hear in *Modern Painters*, writes:

Whatever the value of psychotherapy, and whatever the therapeutic value of self-expression, we have to be clear that no work
of art is reducible to self-expression or justifiable as therapy. For
something to count as art, or to be interesting otherwise than as
a symptom, there has first to be communicative intent on the
part of the artist. He or she has to intend that those who per-
ceive the work should understand what it is he or she is communicating by recognising that the artist is intending to create a
work of art. Art is thus self-consciously communicative in a way
the pure self-expression of a cry of pain or a leap of joy is not,
and intends to communicate as a work of art, not as a description of a patient's symptoms, say.

For many, these exercises are important at a therapeutic level, a
journey of personal discovery, but what they are doing is not art,
not theatre. Sometimes, of course, especially with someone who is
a natural performer, a work can spring forth in its entirety, as in
the case of Kaizaad and the bamboo poles exercise, which he was
able to repeat the following day with the same detail, structure,
rhythm and intensity of feeling. Thus his ritual became a piece of
theatre. And all sacred ritual is theatre, and also, as I have found
when working with professional performers, these exercises can
lead to ritual theatre.

Once a theme or a central image has been found, each successive
improvisation becomes a fresh exploration of that theme, a further
development of the central image, be it that of a wounded foot or
living in an alien culture. Gradually, through repeated work, layer
by layer, detail by detail, the final ritual is crystallized, as in the
example of Carolyn Gracey with which this book commenced.

Each one of us has a seed of life within us which must create the
form or body that will be its inevitable fulfilment, like those multi-
hued seashells, each of which is unique, which the sea animal
creates to house most perfectly its own particular spark of life.
Each one of us has our own myth to live and if we are to achieve
this then we need the same courage that the professional artist
requires in order to realize his or her vision. The spiritual process
exactly mirrors the creative one.

It is significant that, in the West especially, many more people spend large sums of money attending day and weekend (and even longer) courses on different kinds of chanting, meditation and other alternative, holistic practices. Much of this activity reaches loony proportions, spawning religions of ego, but underneath this movement there lies, indisputably, a hunger and a need for rituals that will enshrine the fears, yearnings and conflicts of today. This may also explain why many theatre groups are turning towards the East and those myths which the West has abandoned. People are yearning for a richness and a meaning to life. It may well be that the next major development in theatre will be in the rediscovery of ritual.

Once, in New York, a group of business executives were taking part in a workshop led by a therapist. Each was invited to imagine himself as a tree, growing from seed, and to identify with the life of that tree. At the end of the exercise they were invited to speak about the experience. One of the men described how he had not known what tree he was meant to be and so he lay curled up, imagining himself as a seed, waiting to discover what kind of a tree he would grow into. He never got beyond that stage. Clearly the visualization had resulted in his having to face up to the fact that he had not yet found his true direction in life, and that it was only by being still and waiting that he might hope to find, eventually, in what direction he should be going.

Society can only be renewed by renewing individuals. And in order to do this we have to give individuals an opportunity to contact their own inner resources. As Ira Progoff has remarked,

> We gradually discover that our life has been going somewhere, however blind we have been to its direction, and however unhelpful to it we ourselves have been. We find that a connective thread has been forming beneath the surface of our lives, carrying the meaning that has been trying to establish itself in our existence. It is the inner continuity of our lives. As we recognise and identify with it, we see an inner myth that has been guiding our lives unknown to ourselves.

The value of the exercises described in this book is that each provides a form of self-testing and reveals to us the inner movement within each of us, drawing us towards wholeness, if we will

only allow it. We are seeking the seed of our true Self, the person
we are meant to be, that which is unique to us. We can, and indeed
must, work on our own, but we need also support of others, which
is why people attend workshops. 'This active quality of many
working together,' says Progoff, 'each in his own depths, each
giving his silent and psychic support to those around him, is a
great source of psychic energy. In an intangible way it generates a
power very much as prayer does.' Sometimes an individual's response to one of these exercises is like a map of their life, pointing
the direction in which that person is to go, but it is achieved in the
presence of others who are silent but attentive witnesses to what
has been revealed. It is a work of self-healing, as D. H. Lawrence
describes in his poem, *Healing*:

> I am not a mechanism, an assembly of various sections.
> And it is not because the mechanism is working wrongly
>   that I am ill.
> I am ill because of wounds to the soul, to the deep emotional
>   self –
> And the wounds to the soul take a long, long time,
>   only time can help
> and patience, and a certain difficult repentance,
> long difficult repentance, realisation of life's
> mistake, and the freeing oneself
> from the endless repetition of the mistake
> which mankind at large has chosen to sanctify.

Bibliography

INTRODUCTION

Trollope, Joanna, *The Rector's Wife*, Bloomsbury, 1991.
Turner, Victor, *From Ritual to Theatre*, Performing Arts Journal Publications 1982.
Stevens, Anthony, *On Jung*, Routledge, 1990.

CHAPTER 1

Stevens, Anthony, *Friends and Enemies*, Unpublished play.
Eliade, Mircea, *Ordeal by Labyrinth*, (trans. Derek Coltman), University of Chicago Press, 1982.
Zolla, Elémire, *The Uses of the Imagination and the Decline of the West*, Golgonooza Press, 1978.
Stevens, Anthony, *On Jung*.
Campbell, Joseph, From an article by Kenneth Cavander: 'Heroes when we need them', *American Theatre Journal*, Feb. 1985.
Luke, M. Helen, *Old Age*, Parabola Books, 1987.
Van Gennep, Arnold, *Rites of Passage*, University of Chicago Press, 1908.
Stevens, Anthony, *Archetype*, Routledge and Kegan Paul, 1982.
Bly, Robert, *Iron John*, Element Books, 1991.
Cox, Harvey, *Seduction of the Spirit*, Simon and Schuster, 1973.
Eliade, op. cit.
Gibran, Kahlil, *The Prophet*, Heinemann, 1926.
Sarton, May, *As We Are Now*, Women's Press, 1983.
Roose-Evans, James, *Inner Journey, Outer Journey*, Rider, 1987. (Published in the US under the title, *The Inner Stage*, The Cowley Press, 1990.)
Shorter, Bani, *An Image Darkly Forming*, Routledge, 1990.
Abhishiktananda, *Prayer*, ISPCK, 1975.
Shorter, Bani, *If Ritual Dies*, Guild of Pastoral Psychology, 1989. Guild Lecture No. 231.
Hannah, Barbara, *Jung: His Life and Work, a biographical memoir*, Michael Joseph, 1977.

CHAPTER 2

Shorter, Bani, *An Image Darkly Forming.*
Oida, Yoshi, *An Actor Adrift*, (trans. Lorna Marshall, Foreword by Peter Brook) Methuen, 1992.
Kline, Sally, *Women, Celibacy and Passion*, Andre Deutsch, 1993.
Mansfield, Katherine, *Journal of Katherine Mansfield 1904–1922*, (ed. John Middleton Murry), Hutchinson, New Zealand, 1984.
Turner, Victor. op, cit.

CHAPTER 3

Tara Tulku Rinpoche, quoted in *The Tablet*, 16 June 1990, from an article by Mary Craig, 'A Catholic Buddhist'.
Davies, J.G., *Pilgrimage Yesterday and Today*, SCM Press, 1988.
Duffy, Eamon, *The Tablet*, an article, date and title lost.
Galland, China, *Longing for Darkness*, Century, 1990.
Young, Marjorie S., *Journeys to Glory*, Harper and Row, 1976.
Blacker, Carmen, *The Catalpa Bow*, Allen and Unwin, 1975.

CHAPTER 4

Roose-Evans, James, *Experimental Theatre*, 4th edition, Routledge, 1989.
Bowra, C.M., *Primitive Song*, Weidenfeld & Nicolson, 1962.
William, David (ed.), *Peter Brook: A Theatre Casebook*, Methuen, 1987.

CHAPTER 5

Hesse, Hermann, *The Glass Bead Game*, Holt Rinehart & Winston, 1969.
Raine, Kathleen, *India Seen Afar*, Green Books, 1990.
Cafavy, 'Ithaca', in *Collected Poems*, Chatto and Windus, 1990.
Frost, Robert, 'The Road Not Taken', *The Collected Poems*, Cape, 1971.
Roose-Evans, James, *Inner Journey, Outer Journey*, Rider, 1987. (Published in US under the title *The Inner Stage*, The Crowley Press, 1990.)

CHAPTER 6

Sacks, Oliver, *The Man Who Mistook His Wife For A Hat*, Duckworth, 1983.
Walsh, Christopher, *English Catholic Worship*, a symposium, source untraced.
Munro, Eleanor, *On Glory Roads*, Thames & Hudson, 1987.
Turner, op. cit.

Herriott, John. X., *The Tablet*, 3 March, 1990.
Abhishiktananda, *The Secret of Arunachala*, ISPCK, 1979.
Mehta, P.D., *The Heart of Religion*, Compton Russell, 1978.
Van der Post, Laurens (and Jane Taylor), *Testament to the Bushmen*, Viking Penguin, 1984.
Walker, Barbara, *Women's Rituals*, Harper & Row, 1990.

CHAPTER 7

Auden, W.H., 'O Let Not Time Deceive You', *The Collected Poems*, Faber, 1991.
Sacks, Oliver, source unknown.
King, Joan, 'Saying Goodbye', *The Guardian*, May 23, 1991.
Pincus, Lily, *Death and the Family: the Importance of Mourning*, Faber, 1976.
Jung, C.G., Memories, Dreams and Reflections, Collins, 1963.
Hare, Augustus, *The Story of My Life*, in 6 volumes; first 3 volumes published 1896, the remainder in 1900.
Newell, Venetia, *An Egg At Easter*, Routledge & Kegan Paul, 1971.
Evans-Wentz, W.Y. (ed.) *The Tibetan Book of the Dead*, Oxford University Press, 1980.
Blacker, op. cit.
Sogyal, Rinpoche, *The Tibetan Book of Living and Dying*, Rider, 1992.
Cistercian Studies, journal, date and issue unknown.
The Epic of Gilgamesh, English version by N.K. Sandars, Penguin Classics, 1960.
'Crossing the Bridge at Death', from *The Psychology of Ritual* by Murry Hope, Element, 1988.
Jung, op. cit.
Harvey, Andrew, *A Journey in Ladakh*, Fontana, 1984.
Blacker, Carmen, op. cit.
Chadwick, Richard. 'Our First Lighthouse Funeral', *Leading Lights*, newsletter of the London Lighthouse, Issue No. 2., April 1987.
Lamerton, Richard, *Care of the Dying*, Penguin, 1990.
Sogyal, Rinpoche. op. cit.
Frost, Robert, 'Reluctance', *The Poetry of Robert Frost*, Holt, 1979.
Bly, op. cit.
Frost, Robert, 'The Oven Bird', *The Poetry of Robert Frost*, Holt, 1979.

CHAPTER 8

Turner, op. cit.
Grisbrooke, Bill Jardine, *Liturgical Reform, Liturgical Renewal?*, source untraced.
Young, op. cit.

Plaskow, Judith, 'Bringing a Daughter into the Covenant', from *Woman Spirit Rising*, a feminist reader in religion, edited by Carol P. Christ and Judith Plaskow, Harper Collins, 1979.
Rabbi Schachter-Shalomi, Zalman, *Spiritual Eldering Project*, publicity material, 7318 Hermantown Avenue, Philadelphia, PA19119, USA.
Christ, Carol P., 'Why Women Need the Goddess', from *Woman Spirit Rising*.
Driver, Tom, *The Magic of Ritual*, Harper, 1992.
Moore, Sebastian, and Maguire, Kevin, *The Dreamer, Not the Dream*, Darton, Longman and Todd, 1970.
Zolla, op. cit.

CHAPTER 9

Campbell, Joseph, *The Man with a Thousand Faces*, Grafton, 1988.

EXERCISES

Read, Herbert, *The Cult of Sincerity*, Faber, 1968.
Heilpern, John, *Conference of the Birds*, Faber, 1977.
Smith, Huston. 'Can One Voice Sing a Chord?' *Boston Sunday Globe*, Jan 26 1969.
Lissner, *Man, God and Magic*, Cape, 1961.
Murdoch, Iris, *An Accidental Man*, Chatto & Windus, 1987.
Frost, Robert, 'The Road Not Taken', *The Poetry of Robert Frost*, Holt, 1971.
Frost, Robert. 'The Armful', *The Poetry of Robert Frost*.
Auster, Paul, *Moon Palace*, Faber, 1990.
Campbell, Joseph, with Moyers, Bill, *The Power of Myth*, Doubleday, New York, 1988.
Roose-Evans, James, *Experimental Theatre*.

EPILOGUE

Progoff, Ira, *A Journal Workshop*, Dialogue House Library, New York, 1975.
Lawrence, D.H., 'Healing', *The Collected Poems*, Viking, 1964.